The Book of Enoch & The Fallen Angels

Ancient Secrets from Enoch, Noah, and the Lost Angelic Rebellion That Changed the Bible

A Modern Translation
Adapted for the Contemporary Reader

Various Ancient Jewish Writers (Primarily attributed to Enoch and later scribes)

Translated by Tim Zengerink

Table Of Contents

Preface - Message to the Reader

What If You Could Help Rebuild the Greatest Library in Human History?

Thousands of years ago, the Library of Alexandria stood as the crown jewel of human achievement — a sanctuary where the collected wisdom of every known civilization was gathered, preserved, and shared freely.

And then, it was lost.

Through fire, conquest, and the slow erosion of time, humanity lost not just books — but ideas, dreams, discoveries, and stories that could have changed the world forever.

Today, the Library of Alexandria lives again — and you are invited to be a part of its restoration.

Our mission is simple yet profound:

To rebuild the greatest library the world has ever known, and to translate all timeless works into every language and dialect, so that no seeker of knowledge is ever left behind again.

By joining our movement to rebuild the modern Library of Alexandria, you become part of an unprecedented mission:

- **Unlimited Access to the Greatest Audiobooks & eBooks Ever Written:**

  Instantly explore thousands of legendary works—Plato, Shakespeare, Jane Austen, Leo Tolstoy, and countless more. All instantly available to read or listen, placing a complete literary universe at your fingertips.

- **Beautiful Paperback & Deluxe Editions at Printing Cost**

  Own any title as an elegant paperback, deluxe hardcover, or stunning collectible boxset—offered to you at true printing cost, delivered straight to your door. Build your personal Library of Alexandria, crafted for beauty, built for durability, and worthy of proud display.

- **Fresh Translations for Modern Readers—in Every Language & Dialect**

  Enjoy timeless masterpieces reimagined in clear, contemporary language—no more outdated phrases or obscure references. Alongside the original versions, we're tirelessly translating these classics into every language and dialect imaginable, ensuring accessibility and understanding across cultures and generations.

- **Join a Global Renaissance of Literature & Knowledge**

  You directly support expanding our library, publishing deluxe editions at true cost, translating works into all global languages, and bringing humanity's greatest stories to people everywhere. By joining today, you're not just preserving a legacy of masterpieces; you set in motion a powerful wave of literary accessibility.

Become a Torchbearer of Knowledge.

Join us for free now at **LibraryofAlexandria.com**

Together, we will ensure that the light of human wisdom never fades again.

With gratitude and a shared love of knowledge,

The Modern Library of Alexandria Team

Visit:

www.libraryofalexandria.com

Or scan the code below:

Introduction

Ancient Rebellion, Eternal Consequences

Long before the Book of Genesis offered its brief and cryptic account of "the sons of God" taking "daughters of men," a far more detailed and explosive narrative was being preserved in the shadows of Jewish apocalyptic tradition. This narrative—vivid, disturbing, and cosmically significant—is found in The Book of Enoch and the related texts that trace the story of the Watchers, their forbidden descent to Earth, and the creation of monstrous beings known as the Nephilim. These writings, long excluded from mainstream Bibles, tell a story of divine rebellion that shook the heavens, corrupted the Earth, and forever changed the spiritual and moral condition of humanity.

The Book of Enoch & The Fallen Angels presents this ancient tradition in a unified and accessible form. It is more than a supplement to scripture—it is a revelation of what was once feared, banned, and buried. The texts within, including The Book of the Watchers, The Dream Visions, The Book of the Heavenly Luminaries, The Book of Giants, The Fragments of Noah, and The Testament of Amram, tell a coherent and profound story that influenced everything from early Christianity to Gnostic mysticism, from the Qumran scrolls to modern demonology.

At the heart of this story is Enoch, a mysterious figure from Genesis 5:24—"Enoch walked with God, and he was not, for God took him." In the texts attributed to him, Enoch is no longer just a pious man who vanished mysteriously; he becomes a prophet, scribe of heaven, and intermediary between the divine realm and a corrupted Earth. His role is to bear witness to the crimes of the Watchers, deliver the divine verdict, and receive visions of cosmic justice yet to come.

Through Enoch's eyes, we see the drama unfold: angels lusting after human women, forbidden knowledge unleashed upon the world, the birth of giants who consume all living things, and the eventual descent of divine wrath in the form of the great flood.

The Watchers, also called the "Grigori," are portrayed not merely as rebels, but as cosmic transgressors who blur the line between heaven and Earth. Their sin is not only lust—it is the dissemination of forbidden knowledge. They teach humanity the arts of war, sorcery, astrology, seduction, and alchemy—powers that were meant to remain hidden in the celestial vaults. This is not a story of human fallenness alone; it is a cosmic contagion that begins in the heavens and spreads through the Earth like wildfire.

The consequences of this fall are devastating. The Nephilim—the offspring of angelic fathers and human mothers—become monstrous giants, devouring the Earth's resources and turning against both humans and angels. Their insatiable hunger and violence create a crisis that cannot be ignored by the divine council. Enoch is summoned to deliver a message of judgment: the Watchers will be bound, the Nephilim destroyed, and the world cleansed by a flood that will wipe away the evidence of this forbidden union. But their punishment is not annihilation—it is eternal imprisonment in the abyss, to await the final judgment at the end of days.

Hidden Texts, Revealed Truths

The texts collected in this volume are drawn from various ancient sources, including the Ethiopic Book of Enoch (1 Enoch), fragments discovered among the Dead Sea Scrolls, and lesser-known apocryphal writings such as The Book of Giants and The Testament of Amram. Together, they form a multidimensional account of one of the most suppressed stories in biblical tradition. While these writings were excluded from the canonical Hebrew Bible and later from most

Christian Bibles, they were considered sacred by many early Jewish and Christian communities. The Epistle of Jude, for example, quotes directly from 1 Enoch, and early Church Fathers like Tertullian, Justin Martyr, and Irenaeus affirmed its importance.

Why, then, was this story lost—or more accurately, hidden? The answer lies in its power. The narrative of the Watchers challenges theological boundaries. It raises questions about the origin of evil, the nature of divine justice, and the porous boundary between the spiritual and material worlds. It speaks of angels not as flawless beings of light but as moral agents capable of rebellion. It presents knowledge as both gift and curse. And it suggests that the roots of human suffering extend far beyond Eden.

Modern readers will find in these texts not only mythological fascination, but theological depth. The fallen angels represent more than supernatural villains—they symbolize the seduction of power, the danger of transgressing sacred boundaries, and the consequences of misusing divine gifts. The Nephilim, in turn, are not just monstrous hybrids—they are the embodiment of imbalance, violence, and unchecked desire. Enoch's visions offer both comfort and warning: God sees all, judges righteously, and promises to restore balance to a world that has been thrown into chaos.

This modern adaptation preserves the dramatic and poetic force of the original texts while translating them into contemporary language that retains their mystery and spiritual gravitas. The goal is not to sensationalize these writings, but to honor them—to give them the clarity, dignity, and accessibility they deserve. Where possible, historical and theological notes have been included to help modern readers navigate the complex symbolism and cosmology of these ancient works.

The Book of Enoch & The Fallen Angels is an invitation to recover what was lost, to rethink the familiar, and to reimagine the sacred. It is a book for scholars and seekers, skeptics and believers—for anyone who suspects that the Bible we inherited is only part of the story.

May these texts open your eyes to the deeper battle between light and darkness. May they awaken your spirit to the mysteries of creation, rebellion, and redemption. And may they challenge you to walk, like Enoch, not in fear of the fallen—but in communion with the divine, even amid a world that has forgotten its origins.

The Book of The Watchers

The Book of the Watchers, the first section of 1 Enoch, is an important text in apocalyptic literature. It tells the story of the Watchers, a group of angels who came down to earth, married human women, and shared forbidden knowledge with people. Their actions led to corruption and chaos, which eventually brought divine judgment.

At the center of the story is Enoch, a righteous man chosen to witness the heavenly realms and deliver God's message of judgment to the rebellious Watchers. The book explores themes of divine justice, the balance of the universe, and the boundaries between heaven and earth.

The Book of the Watchers is a key part of 1 Enoch and has greatly influenced discussions about angels, sin, and the origins of evil. It has shaped both Jewish and Christian teachings, and its powerful imagery and moral lessons continue to inspire readers.

The Words of the Blessing

These are the words of the blessing that Enoch spoke to the righteous, the chosen ones who will live during a time of great trouble. In that time, all their enemies will be removed, and the righteous will be saved.

Introduction
An Oracle of Judgment (1:2—5:9)

And he started his message, saying:

"Enoch was a good man, and God helped him see clearly. He was shown a vision of the Holy One and heaven, and it was revealed to me as well. I heard everything from the watchers and the holy ones, and as

I listened, I began to understand what I had seen.

This message is not for the people living now, but for those in a distant future.

Now, I will speak about those who have been chosen, because this message is meant for them."

PE Peophany

The Great Holy One will step out from His home,
and the eternal God will descend to stand on Mount Sinai.
He will come with His mighty army,
surrounded by countless powerful beings from heaven.

All the watchers will be filled with fear,
and those hiding in distant places will lift their voices in song.
The whole earth will shake violently,   .
and terror will spread even to the farthest lands.

The highest mountains will tremble and break apart,
the tall hills will collapse and melt like wax in a fire.
The earth itself will be torn apart,
and everything on it will be destroyed, for judgment is coming to
     all.

But for those who do what is right, He will bring peace.
He will protect His chosen ones and surround them with mercy.
They will belong fully to Him, and He will take joy in them.
He will bless them, help them, and shine His light upon them.

Look, He is coming with countless holy ones,
to bring judgment upon the world,

to remove all who do evil,
and to hold everyone accountable for their wrong actions
and for the arrogant and cruel words that sinners have spoken
 against Him.

PE Indictmenta

Think about all of His works and the wonders of the sky. Notice how the heavens move exactly as they should, how the stars and lights in the sky rise and set at their proper times. Each one follows its path, marking the seasons and special days without ever changing from the order set for them.

Now, look at the earth and the amazing things that have happened on it since creation. Nothing truly changes because everything follows God's plan, steady and unshaken.

Pay attention to the seasons, the signs of summer and winter. Think about winter—how the ground becomes soaked with water, the sky fills with clouds, and rain and dew fall to nourish the land.

See how, in winter, most trees seem lifeless, their leaves dried up and gone. But there are fourteen trees that are different. They hold onto their old leaves until, after two or three years, new ones finally grow.

Now, think about the signs of summer. The sun shines with intense heat, burning the earth. You search for shade to escape its strength, while the ground becomes so hot that even the dust and stones seem to burn beneath your feet.

Look at the trees in summer. Their leaves grow thick and green, covering the branches. Their fruit ripens in abundance, adding beauty and richness to the land.

When you see these wonders, remember that the One who lives forever created them all. Year after year, His works remain the same, each one serving its purpose just as He planned. Everything follows His command without fail.

Just as the sky and the earth obey Him, so do the seas and rivers. They continue their work without change, carrying out their tasks exactly as He directed.

But people have not remained faithful. They have turned away from His ways and ignored His commands. Instead, they have spoken with pride and arrogance, using their words to challenge His power.

You who are stubborn in your hearts—there will be no peace for you!

PE Verdict

Your life will be filled with regret, and the years you've lived will feel meaningless. The time of your downfall will turn into an endless curse, with no mercy or peace for you.

Your names will be remembered as a warning to others, and people will use them in their curses. The wicked will swear by your names, but those who are chosen will celebrate. They will receive forgiveness, kindness, and peace in abundance.

A bright light will shine on those who are chosen, and they will inherit the earth with happiness and peace. But for sinners, there will be no rescue—only a lasting curse.

The righteous will live in joy, surrounded by light and peace, while the wicked will face only misfortune.

Wisdom will be given to the chosen ones, and they will live without sin, free from arrogance and disbelief. They will gain understanding, and their minds will be filled with truth. They will no longer turn toward wrongdoing or disobey what is right.

They will not be destroyed by God's anger. Instead, they will live out their full days in peace, filled with joy, and they will remain in happiness forever.

The Rebellion of The Watchers (Chapters 6–11)

PE Conspiracy

As more people were born on the earth, many daughters grew up to be beautiful and attractive. The watchers, who were beings from the heavens, saw them and were overcome with desire. They said to each other, "Let's choose wives from among these women and have children with them."

Their leader, Shemihazah, warned them, "I'm afraid that you might change your minds, and I'll be the only one left to take the blame for this great sin."

But they all reassured him, saying, "Let's make a promise together and bind ourselves with a curse, so that no one backs out. We will go through with our plan no matter what."

So they swore an oath as a group and sealed it with a curse. There were two hundred of them in total, and they came down to earth during the time of Jared, landing on the top of Mount Hermon. They named the mountain "Hermon" because that was where they made their oath and bound themselves under the curse.

These were the names of their leaders: Shemihazah was their chief. Arteqoph was second, followed by Remashel, Kokabel, Armumahel, Ramel, Daniel, Ziqel, Baraqel, Asael, Hermani, Matarel, Ananel, Setawel, Samshiel, Sahriel, Tummiel, Turiel, Yamiel, and Yehadiel. These were the leaders of their groups.

PE Deed and Its Results

The watchers, along with those who followed them, chose wives from among human women, taking whoever they wanted. They lived with them, corrupting themselves through these relationships, and taught them things that were never meant to be known. They revealed the secrets of magic and spells and showed them how to use plants and roots for forbidden purposes.

The women became pregnant and gave birth to massive giants. These giants later had children of their own, called the Nephilim, and from the Nephilim came another generation known as the Elioud. Each new generation grew even larger and stronger.

The giants began taking everything that humans worked hard to produce, but no matter how much they took, it was never enough. When food ran out, they turned to violence, killing people to survive. Their evil only grew worse—they started harming birds, animals, and even fish, eating their flesh and drinking their blood.

The earth itself could no longer endure their cruelty, and it cried out against them.

PE Secrets the Watchers Reveal

Asael taught people how to make weapons, showing them how to forge swords from iron and craft shields, armor, and other tools for battle. He also introduced them to the metals found in the earth, teaching them how to shape gold into jewelry and silver into bracelets and decorations for women. He even showed them how to use antimony for makeup, craft beautiful stones, and create colorful dyes.

People eagerly used this knowledge, making weapons and ornaments for themselves and their daughters. But with this new knowledge, they strayed from the right path, leading others away from what was holy. Wickedness spread quickly, and humanity became more corrupt.

Shemihazah taught the secrets of spells and how to use plants for magic. Hermani revealed sorcery, ways to break spells, and other magical practices. Baraqel explained how to interpret lightning, while Kokabel taught about the stars. Ziqel showed the meaning of shooting stars, Arteqoph revealed signs from the earth, Shamsiel taught the movement of the sun, and Sahriel explained the phases of the moon.

These watchers shared their forbidden knowledge with their wives and children, revealing mysteries that were never meant to be known. As humanity became more corrupt, suffering and death increased. The cries of those in pain reached up to the heavens.

PE Intercession of The Four Archangels

Michael, Sariel, Raphael, and Gabriel looked down from the heights of heaven and saw the earth covered in violence and bloodshed. Wickedness had spread everywhere, corrupting the land.

They turned to one another and said, "The earth is filled with suffering, and the cries of the innocent rise up to heaven. The souls of those who have been wronged call out to us, pleading, 'Take our case before the Most High. Bring justice for our destruction before the Lord, the ruler of all.'"

They approached the presence of the Eternal Lord and said, "You are the God above all, the King of kings, the everlasting ruler of every age. Your throne stands firm from the beginning of time and will last forever. Your name is holy, great, and blessed for all eternity.

"You created everything, and your power rules over all that exists. Nothing is hidden from you—every action, every secret is laid bare before your eyes. You see all things, and nothing escapes your knowledge.

"You have seen what Asael has done. He has revealed forbidden secrets to humanity—mysteries that were meant to stay hidden in heaven. Because of him, people have fallen deeper into sin, chasing after knowledge they were never meant to have.

"Shemihazah, whom you placed in charge of his followers, has also disobeyed you. He and his companions have taken human women for themselves, lying with them and corrupting them with sin. They have taught them sorcery and charms that spread hatred and destruction.

"The women have given birth to their children—giants, born from both heaven and earth. These creatures have filled the world with violence, spilling innocent blood and spreading wickedness across the land.

"The souls of those who have died cry out to you without rest. Their voices rise to heaven, pleading for justice against the sins that have overtaken the earth.

"Lord, you know all things before they even happen. You have seen all of this unfold, yet you have not told us what must be done. How should we bring justice for the wrongs that have been committed?"

PE Commissioning of The Four Archangels

The Most High spoke, and the Great Holy One made His decision known. He sent Sariel to deliver a message to Noah, the son of Lamech.

"Go to Noah and tell him in My name, 'Take shelter.' Warn him that the end is near, and the whole earth will be destroyed. A great flood is coming—a massive storm that will sweep across the land and wipe out all life. Teach this righteous man, the son of Lamech, what he must do to survive and escape this disaster. From him, a new generation will rise, one that will last for all time."

Then the Lord gave Raphael a command: "Raphael, go and capture Asael. Tie his hands and feet, and throw him into the darkness. Make an opening in the desert at Doudael, cast him inside, and place sharp, jagged stones beneath him. Cover him in darkness, so he will never see the light again. He will remain there for a long time, until the great day of judgment, when he will be thrown into the fire.

Heal the earth, which has been ruined by the Watchers, and restore it so that humanity does not perish because of the forbidden knowledge they passed down. The world was left in chaos because of Asael's teachings, and his sins must be recorded against him."

The Lord then turned to Gabriel and said, "Gabriel, go and deal with the children born from these forbidden unions—the hybrids, the offspring of the Watchers. Let them turn against each other and destroy themselves in a great war. They will not live long lives, and their fathers' pleas will not be heard. They will have no hope for eternal life, and none of them will live beyond five hundred years."

Finally, He spoke to Michael: "Michael, capture Shemihazah and all those who took human women as their own and corrupted themselves with them. When their sons have been destroyed and they have seen the loss of their loved ones, bind these Watchers and imprison them in the depths of the earth for seventy generations. They will remain there until the day of their judgment and final punishment.

On that day, they will be thrown into the fire, where they will suffer forever. All those who are condemned will be bound together with them until their time is finished. When judgment comes, they will be erased from existence for all eternity. Destroy the spirits of the hybrids and the sons of the Watchers, for they have brought suffering to humanity and ruin to the earth."

Michael Is to Renovate the Earth

Remove every trace of evil from the earth, wiping out all acts of wrongdoing completely. Let goodness and truth grow strong, like a thriving plant, bringing blessings to everyone. Righteousness and honesty will take root forever, filling the world with joy and peace.

During this time, all who live righteously will be safe. They will enjoy long, full lives, growing in number, and both the young and old will live in peace, without fear or trouble.

The whole earth will be transformed into a paradise, filled with trees and overflowing with blessings. Every joyful tree will be planted, and vineyards will cover the land. Each vine will produce a thousand jugs of wine, and every seed planted will bring an incredible harvest. Olive trees will be abundant, producing more oil than ever before.

The world will be cleansed of every impurity, injustice, and sin. All corruption and wrongdoing that once polluted the earth will be completely wiped away.

Then, humanity itself will be changed. People will choose to live righteously, and all nations will worship and honor their Creator. They will praise His name and show Him respect and devotion.

The earth will be purified, free from anything unclean or corrupt. Never again will disaster or punishment come upon its people for all future generations.

At that time, the heavens will open and pour out blessings upon the world, enriching the work of human hands.

Truth and peace will stand together, side by side, lasting forever. These gifts will remain for all generations, bringing eternal harmony and prosperity to humankind.

Enoch's Interaction with The Fallen Watchers (Chapters 12–16)

An Editorial Introduction

Before all these things happened, Enoch disappeared, and no one knew where he had gone or what had happened to him. His life was deeply connected to the watchers, and he spent his days among the holy ones.

Enoch's First Mission to The Fallen Watchers

Enoch Is Sent to the Watchers

I, Enoch, stood in awe, praising the Lord of majesty, the eternal King. Suddenly, the watchers of the Great Holy One called out to me, addressing me as Enoch the scribe. They said,

"Enoch, righteous scribe, go and deliver a message to the watchers of heaven—those who abandoned their sacred home and corrupted themselves by being with human women. Like the men of earth, they took wives for themselves, bringing great destruction upon the world.

Tell them, 'You will have no peace and no forgiveness. As for your children, whom you cherish—you will see them destroyed.
You will mourn their loss,
and though you beg for mercy, none will be given to you.'

Enoch, also take this message to Asael: 'There will be no peace for you. A harsh judgment has been decided against you, and you will be bound. No relief or forgiveness will come for the evil you revealed—the corruption, sin, and lawlessness you taught to humanity.'"

Then I went and delivered this message to all of them together. When they heard it, they were overcome with fear, trembling as terror filled them.

Pe Fallen Watchers Commission Enoch to Intercede For Pem

They begged me to write a request on their behalf, a petition that might bring them forgiveness. They wanted me to bring it before the Lord of heaven. They were so ashamed of what they had done and the punishment they faced that they couldn't even look up toward heaven or speak for themselves.

I wrote down their plea, listing each of their requests, along with the details of their actions. They also asked for mercy for their children, hoping they would be allowed to live longer. After finishing the petition, I traveled to the waters of Dan, in the land of Dan, west of Mount Hermon. There, I sat down and read their plea aloud to God.

As I prayed for them, the weight of their words and my responsibility became too much, and I eventually fell asleep.

Enoch's Ascent to Heaven And Second Commission To Preach to The Watchers

Narrative Summary

As I rested, vivid dreams filled my mind, and visions overwhelmed me like a rushing flood. I saw images of judgment and wrath, and in the midst of them, a powerful voice commanded, "Go to the watchers and deliver a message of warning." When I woke up, I immediately set out to find them.

I came upon the watchers, gathered in sorrow at Abel Main, a place between Lebanon and Senir. They sat together, weeping bitterly, their faces covered in shame. Standing before them, I recounted every vision I had seen in my dream. I spoke the words of truth and the warning I had been given to deliver.

This is the record, written as The Book of the Words of Truth and the Warning to the Watchers Who Have Been Here Since Ancient Times, as commanded by the Great Holy One in my dream. I share what I saw with my human voice, using the breath the Creator has given mankind for speech and understanding. Just as He created people to comprehend wisdom, He chose me to deliver this message to the watchers, the sons of heaven.

I wrote down your petition as you requested, but in the vision, it was made clear—your request will not be granted. Not now, not ever.

Judgment has been made, and you will never return to heaven again. You will remain bound to the earth forever.

But before this happens, you will witness the destruction of your children, those you love most. You will watch as they are killed, and their deaths will bring you no comfort. You will beg for mercy, but none will come. No part of the petition I wrote will be fulfilled.

In the vision, I saw more: clouds gathered, calling out to me, and mist rose up, summoning me. Shooting stars and flashes of lightning pulled me forward, carrying me upward. Powerful winds lifted me from all directions, raising me into the heavens.

I arrived at a massive wall, shining like ice, surrounded by tongues of fire that flickered and danced. Fear gripped me, but I pressed on and stepped into the flames.

Inside, I saw an enormous and magnificent house, made entirely of glistening ice. The walls were bright and white like snow, and the floor beneath me was pure ice. Above, the ceiling sparkled with the brilliance of shooting stars and flashes of lightning. Fiery beings moved through the space, and the sky itself looked like flowing water. A ring of fire surrounded the entire structure, and the doors burned with an unquenchable flame.

I entered, but the place was filled with extremes—burning heat like fire and freezing cold like ice. It was unlike anything I had ever known, lifeless and overwhelming. Fear took hold of me, and I began to tremble. My strength left me, and I collapsed, my face to the ground.

Then I saw something even greater: another house, far more magnificent than the first. It was built entirely of fire, radiating a brilliance beyond words. The entire floor burned with flames, and the upper portion flashed with lightning and shooting stars. Even the ceiling was covered in fire, filling the space with an overwhelming presence.

As I looked further, I saw a towering throne. It shined like crystal, and its wheels blazed as bright as the sun. Around it, countless fiery beings sang in harmony. Beneath the throne, rivers of fire flowed endlessly. The sight was beyond my understanding.

Seated on the throne was a figure whose presence lit up everything. His clothing shone like the sun, brighter than the purest snow, and His radiance was unmatched. No angel dared to enter or even look at Him because His brilliance was too overwhelming. No human could withstand His glory. Flames surrounded Him, and a great fire stood beside Him. None of those around Him dared to approach.

Before Him stood countless multitudes—ten thousand times ten thousand—but He needed no advisor, for His very words brought things into existence.

The holy ones closest to Him remained in His presence at all times, never leaving, always devoted to His glory.

As I lay trembling before Him, the Lord suddenly called my name: "Come here, Enoch, and listen to My words."

One of the holy ones came forward, lifted me up, and helped me stand, but I kept my face lowered, unable to look at the One before me.

Then the voice of the Great One spoke again, calming my fear: "Do not be afraid, Enoch, righteous man and scribe of truth. Come closer and hear what I have to say. Go and speak to the watchers who sent you to plead for them. Tell them this:

'It is not for humans to intercede for you; you were meant to intercede for them. Why did you leave the heights of heaven, your eternal home, and defile yourselves with human women? You became like mortal men, taking wives and fathering children—giants born from your union. You were created as spirits, meant to live forever, but you corrupted yourselves with lust, a desire meant only for those who die.

I gave men wives so they could continue their lineage and sustain life on earth. But you—your existence was never meant to rely on such things. Your home was in heaven, not on earth, and I did not create wives for you.

Now, the spirits of the giants—born from the union of heavenly beings and humans—have become evil spirits on the earth. Though they came from human mothers, they are corrupted by the watchers who fathered them. They will remain on earth as wicked spirits, leading people astray.

These spirits will cause violence, destruction, and suffering. They will spread sickness, attack humanity, and bring harm to women. Though they do not eat, they are always hungry, and though they do not drink, they remain thirsty, causing endless misery.

Since the day the giants were killed, their spirits have wandered the earth, bringing destruction without being judged. This will continue until the final day of judgment when all things will be set right.

Now, go and tell the watchers who sent you to plead for them: You once lived in heaven, but you betrayed your place. No secrets were ever entrusted to you, yet you stole forbidden knowledge and taught it to women. Because of this, human wickedness has multiplied, and corruption has spread across the earth.

Tell them plainly: 'You will find no peace.'"

Enoch's Journey to The Northwest (Chapters 17–19)

PE Journey Narrative Begun

They took me to a place unlike anything I had ever seen. The beings who lived there were made of fire, their bodies glowing and burning with an intense energy. Yet, when they wanted to, they could take on human form, hiding their fiery nature. Watching them change left me in awe, for their transformations were beyond anything I could understand.

From there, they led me into deep darkness. Before me stood an enormous mountain, so tall its peak seemed to touch the heavens. Standing at its base, I could feel its power and the mysteries it held. They guided me further, and I saw the realm of the stars and celestial lights. Here were the places where their brightness was stored, along with the chambers of thunder, where powerful roars echoed. The very fabric of the sky was revealed to me, showing bows of fire, flaming arrows, quivers filled with burning shafts, and even a sword made entirely of fire. Flashes of lightning surrounded me, lighting up the darkness with their dazzling brilliance.

Next, they took me to the source of living waters—streams flowing with life and mystery. From there, I was led to a great fire in the west, the force behind the setting sun, painting the sky with its warm, glowing colors every evening. This fire had an everlasting power, its presence felt in the fading light of every day.

Then, I came to a river unlike any other—a river of fire, flowing as freely as water. Its blazing currents rushed downward into a massive sea in the west, where the fiery stream merged with the dark waters, casting a shimmering glow across its surface. It was both breathtaking and terrifying, a reminder of forces far beyond human control.

As my journey continued, I was shown all the great rivers of the earth, their waters winding through the land. Eventually, I reached a powerful river that led into a vast darkness. There was no light, and as I moved forward, I entered a place untouched by human feet. The land was silent, untouched, filled with an eerie stillness.

Here, I saw the cold, howling winds of darkness, relentless and unyielding as they swept through the void. Deep waters gushed from hidden depths, their sources unknown and impossible to understand. I stood before the mouths of all the rivers of the world, each one pouring its waters into this unseen realm. Finally, I arrived at the edge of the abyss itself—a vast, endless chasm, so deep and consuming that it felt like it held the very secrets of creation.

A Digression:
A Summary of What Enoch Saw

I was shown the great storehouses of the winds, vast and complex places where the forces that move the air across the sky and the earth are kept. Through these winds, the Creator brings balance to everything, placing each part of creation exactly where it belongs. Though invisible, their power shapes the natural world, connecting the sky and the land in ways beyond human understanding.

My vision reached the very foundation of the earth, where I saw its mighty cornerstone. It was a structure of unshakable strength, holding all of creation in place. I saw the four great winds that support both the earth and the heavens above. Though unseen, these winds serve as the pillars of the sky, keeping everything in perfect balance.

I watched as the winds stretched high, lifting the heavens and holding them in place. They formed an invisible link between the earth and the sky, creating a bridge that supports the heavens. These winds are the framework upon which the vast sky rests, ensuring harmony between the realms above and below.

I saw how the winds of heaven guided the movements of the celestial bodies. They turned the great circle of the sun, directing it toward its setting with perfect accuracy, and they led the stars on their paths across the night sky. These winds did not move randomly, but followed a set order, their motions controlled by divine wisdom.

Then I looked toward the earth and saw the winds carrying the clouds. Sometimes they moved them gently, while at other times they pushed them forward with great force, spreading rain and shade across the land. I also saw the paths of the angels, moving between the sky and the earth as they carried out their duties. These paths shone brightly and were perfectly ordered, a reflection of their divine purpose.

At last, I reached the farthest edge of the earth, where the sky above formed a great boundary between the land and the heavens. Here, the connection between the earthly and the celestial became clear. It was a breathtaking sight, revealing the beauty of creation and the careful way the heavens and the earth were woven together. I stood in awe, amazed at the infinite power and wisdom of the Creator.

PE Journey Narrative Concluded

I arrived at a place where fire burned without end, day and night. In the midst of this blazing land stood seven enormous mountains made of precious stones, more magnificent than anything I had ever seen. Three were to the east and three to the south, each glowing with an otherworldly beauty.

The eastern mountains shimmered with colors of rare gems—pearl, jasper, and dazzling stones that seemed to shine with life. The mountains to the south glowed with fiery red stones, their surfaces flickering like flames. The tallest mountain among them stretched high into the sky, its peak like a grand throne made of antimony, crowned with a brilliant blue top of lapis lazuli. The entire scene was surrounded by flames that never faded, burning with an intense and sacred fire.

Beyond these mountains, I reached what seemed to be the very edge of the world. Here, the sky met its boundary, and the vast universe appeared to come to an end. A deep chasm lay before me, surrounded by towering pillars of fire. These fiery columns stretched endlessly in both directions—soaring into the sky and plunging into the depths below, lighting up the darkness of the abyss.

Standing beside me, Uriel explained the meaning of this place. "Here," he said, "are the angels who broke the laws of heaven. They took human women as their own and fathered children. Their spirits have changed form many times, bringing destruction to humanity and leading people to worship false gods. They will continue to mislead mankind until the day of final judgment, when they will receive their punishment. Their wives will also suffer for their sins, becoming sirens, forever trapped by their wrongdoing."

Moving past the chasm, I entered a place that felt completely abandoned. There was no sky above and no solid ground below. No water flowed, and no birds flew there. It was an empty void, terrifying in its silence and lifelessness.

In this desolate space, I saw seven stars, burning like massive mountains of fire. I asked the angel with me what they were, and he explained:

"This is the outermost edge of heaven and earth. It is the prison where rebellious stars and heavenly beings are kept. These stars once had a purpose, but they defied the Creator's command. They failed to appear at their appointed times, and because of their disobedience, the Lord has bound them here in fire. They will remain imprisoned until the time of judgment, when their sins will finally be accounted for—ten thousand years from now."

Beyond all these visions, I, Enoch, saw the farthest reaches of creation. No other human has witnessed what I have seen—the ends of the heavens and the earth, the hidden truths of the stars, and the fate of those who fell from grace. These revelations were shown to me alone, revealing the deep and mysterious forces that shape existence.

Enoch's Journey Eastward
(Chapters 20–36)

List of The Seven Archangels

These are the names of the seven holy angels, each given a special duty by the Creator. They watch over the world and carry out God's will with wisdom and care.

Uriel is one of the sacred angels. He is responsible for watching over the world and Tartarus, the deep abyss where rebellious spirits are sent. He ensures that divine justice is carried out, keeping order in both the earth and the underworld.

Raphael is in charge of human souls. He protects and guides them, making sure they follow the path meant for them. He is also known as a healer and guardian, bringing comfort and protection to people.

Reuel is responsible for enforcing justice among the celestial bodies. He ensures that the stars and heavenly lights follow their intended course and that no power is misused.

Michael is the great archangel assigned to protect the righteous. He stands as a leader and defender of those who are faithful, guiding them in their struggles against evil. He is a strong and powerful protector of God's people.

Sariel is given authority over spirits that sin against the spirit. He deals with those who go beyond ordinary wrongdoing, committing offenses that disrupt the divine order. He ensures that they face the consequences of their actions.

Gabriel is the guardian of paradise. He watches over the garden of eternal life, as well as the serpents and cherubim that dwell there. His duty is to keep paradise pure and untouched, making sure it remains a place of divine beauty.

Remiel is the angel responsible for those who rise again. He oversees resurrection, guiding souls as they ascend to their destined place in the divine order.

These seven angels—Uriel, Raphael, Reuel, Michael, Sariel, Gabriel, and Remiel—are the great archangels of the Lord. Each carries out their mission with absolute devotion, ensuring the balance of creation and carrying out God's justice in both heaven and earth. Their names reflect their sacred roles and the divine order established by God.

PE Place of Punishment for
The Disobedient Stars

I traveled to a place filled with disorder and confusion, unlike anything I had ever seen. There was no sky above to bring light or hope, and no solid ground beneath to provide stability. Everything around me felt unstable, as if nothing had a true form or foundation. It was a space of chaos, overwhelming and unsettling.

In the middle of this place, I saw something that filled me with both awe and fear—seven stars, chained together and trapped in this stormy void. They were massive, like towering mountains, and covered in flames that burned endlessly, consuming them without rest.

Shaken by what I saw, I turned and asked, "Why are these stars bound like this? What did they do to deserve such a punishment?"

Uriel, one of the holy angels who was guiding me, stood nearby. He looked at me and replied, "Enoch, why do you seek to understand this? Why do you want to know the reason behind what you see?"

Then he explained their fate to me. "These stars are not just celestial bodies; they were once part of the heavens. But they disobeyed the commands of the Lord, refusing to follow the paths set for them. Because of their rebellion, they have been locked away in this fiery prison. They will remain here for ten thousand years—until the time of their judgment has been fulfilled."

His words weighed heavily on me. I stood in silence, trying to grasp the meaning of what I had witnessed. Around us, the chaos of this place raged like a storm without end.

PE Prison of The Fallen Angels

From there, I was taken to an even more terrifying place than the one before. As I got closer, a deep sense of fear and unease filled me. What I saw was beyond anything I had ever imagined. A massive fire raged, its flames roaring and leaping as if they were alive. This was not an ordinary fire—it moved with power and fury, burning endlessly with an intensity that seemed unnatural.

In this dreadful place, I saw a deep, narrow chasm stretching far into the abyss. Around it stood enormous pillars of fire, each one plunging into the darkness below. The sight was both fascinating and horrifying, as the depth of the abyss and the size of the fiery pillars seemed impossible to measure or fully understand. No matter how hard I tried, I couldn't grasp how vast it truly was—it seemed to stretch on forever, disappearing into the shadows.

Overwhelmed by the horror of what I was witnessing, I cried out, "This place is beyond terrifying! No one should ever have to see something so dreadful!"

At that moment, Uriel, one of the holy angels guiding me, stepped forward. His presence was calm, completely different from the chaos and fear surrounding us. He turned to me and asked, "Enoch, why are you so afraid? Why does this sight shake you so much?"

Still trembling, I answered, "How could I not be? This place is beyond anything I can bear. Just looking at it fills me with fear, and everything about it is horrifying."

Uriel then spoke again, his voice steady and full of authority. "This place is a prison. It is where the rebellious angels have been locked away, and here they will remain forever. Their punishment will never end, and this fiery abyss will be their eternal home."

As I took in his words, I felt the weight of their meaning pressing down on me. This was not just a place of fire and destruction—it was a warning, a symbol of divine justice. The flames and the endless abyss stood as a reminder of the price of disobedience, their presence forever marking the consequences of defying the will of the Almighty.

PE Mountain of The Dead

From there, I was taken to another place, where I saw a huge mountain of solid rock in the west. Inside the mountain were four deep and smooth hollow spaces. Three of them were dark, while one was bright and filled with light. In the center of the bright hollow, a fountain of water flowed.

I looked at the hollows and said, "These spaces are so deep and smooth, but why do they look so dark?"

Then Raphael, one of the holy angels with me, answered, "These hollows were created to hold the spirits of the dead. This is their purpose. Every soul comes here after death. These are the places where they are kept, waiting until the final day of judgment."

As I stood there, I heard the spirit of a man crying out, his voice filled with pain and desperation. His sorrowful cries rose up toward heaven as he pleaded for justice.

I turned to Raphael and asked, "Who is this spirit crying out so desperately?"

Raphael replied, "This is the spirit of Abel, who was killed by his brother Cain. Abel's spirit calls out against Cain and will continue to do so until all of Cain's descendants are wiped from the earth."

Then I asked about the different hollow spaces, wanting to

Translated by Tim Zengerink

understand why they were separated.

Raphael explained, "Each hollow was made for a different group of spirits.

The first hollow, the bright one with the fountain, is for the spirits of the righteous. This is where those who lived good and faithful lives are gathered.

The second hollow is for sinners—those who died without being judged for their wrongdoing while they were alive. Their spirits suffer in this place, waiting for the great day of judgment when they will receive their final punishment. They will remain bound here forever.

The third hollow is for the spirits of those who were murdered. These spirits cry out for justice, revealing the pain and destruction they suffered at the hands of evildoers.

The fourth hollow is for the spirits of the godless—those who lived in sin and walked alongside the wicked. These spirits will never rise again, and they will never receive a second chance at life."

Hearing this, I praised the Lord and said, "Righteous is Your judgment! Blessed are You, Lord of majesty and justice, the eternal ruler of all time!"

PE Fire of The West

From there, I traveled to another place, far to the west at the edge of the earth. I saw a fire that never went out—it burned endlessly, moving day and night without ever stopping.

I asked, "What is this fire that never stops?"

Reuel, one of the holy angels with me, answered, "This is the fire of the west. It follows the paths of the heavenly lights as they move through the sky."

Then he showed me mountains made of fire, burning without end, their flames glowing both day and night.

PE Mountain Of God and
The Tree of Life

I continued my journey and came upon seven magnificent mountains, each unique and dazzling with precious stones. Their beauty was breathtaking, and they shone brightly in the light. Three of them stood to the east, stacked one above the other, and three to the south, also layered the same way. Between them were deep, rugged valleys that never met.

The seventh mountain stood in the center, taller than all the others. It had the shape of a throne, and around it grew many fragrant trees. Among them was one unlike any I had ever seen. Its scent was sweeter than any spice, and its leaves, blossoms, and branches never withered. The fruit it bore looked like dates from palm trees and seemed perfect in every way.

I said, "This tree is incredible! Its fragrance is amazing, its leaves are beautiful, and its blossoms are stunning."

Then Michael, one of the holy angels with me and their leader, spoke and said, "Enoch, why are you so curious about this tree? Why do you wonder about its fragrance and beauty? Do you wish to understand its purpose?"

I replied, "Yes, I want to know everything, but especially about this tree."

Michael answered, "The tall mountain you see, the one shaped like a throne, is where the Great Holy One, the Lord of Glory, the King of Eternity, will sit when He comes to visit the earth with goodness.

As for this special tree, no human may touch it until the great day of judgment, when justice is served, and everything is brought to completion. After that, it will be given to the righteous and the faithful.

They will eat its fruit, and it will be placed near God's holy dwelling, beside the house of the Eternal King.

Then the righteous will rejoice, full of happiness as they enter the holy sanctuary. The tree's fragrance will fill their very bones, and they will live long, joyful lives, just as their ancestors did in the past. They will no longer suffer pain, hardship, or disease."

Hearing this, I praised the God of Glory, the Eternal King, who has prepared such wonderful blessings for the righteous and has promised to share them with His people.

Jerusalem,
The Center of The Earth and
The Place of Punishment

From there, I traveled to the center of the earth, where I saw a beautiful and blessed land. It was filled with trees that stayed green and kept growing without end. In this place, there was also a holy mountain.

From beneath the mountain, a stream of water flowed eastward and continued south. To the east of this mountain, I saw another mountain, even taller, and between the two was a deep, narrow valley with water running beneath the mountain.

To the west of the first mountain, I saw a smaller mountain, not very tall. Below it was a deep, dry valley. Another deep and dry valley lay at the point where the three mountains met. These valleys were carved from solid rock, with no trees or life growing in them.

I was amazed by the sight of the mountains and the valleys, unable to comprehend what I was seeing.

I asked, "Why is this land so blessed, filled with trees, while this valley is barren and lifeless?"

Sariel, one of the holy angels with me, answered, "This valley is cursed. It is meant for those who are condemned forever. It is the place where those who have spoken against the Lord and dishonored His name will be gathered. They will remain here until the final days, when they will face judgment in the presence of the righteous for all eternity. Even in this place, the godless will recognize the Lord's greatness and bless His name.

During their judgment, they will finally understand His mercy and the kindness they were given."

Hearing this, I praised the Lord of glory, declaring His greatness and honoring Him with deep respect.

To The Paradise of Righteousness

I traveled to a mountain range in the middle of the desert. Most of the land was dry and barren, except for one area filled with trees and plants. A large stream of water flowed down from above, spreading like a wide river toward the northwest, carrying water and moisture to the land.

From there, I moved east of the mountains and came to another part of the desert. In the fields, I saw trees that smelled like frankincense and myrrh, and they looked similar to nut trees.

Continuing farther east, I reached a vast land filled with valleys of water. In these valleys, I saw fragrant plants growing, similar to reeds. Along the banks, the air was filled with the sweet scent of cinnamon.

Beyond these valleys, I traveled even farther east and came to another mountain range. The mountains were covered with trees that produced a fragrant nectar called storax and galbanum. Beyond these mountains, I found another covered in aloe trees. These trees were full of sap, and their bark looked like that of almond trees. When ground into powder, the bark released a fragrance sweeter than any perfume.

Continuing to the northeast, I saw more mountains filled with the finest spices—nard, tspr, cardamom, and pepper. From there, I journeyed even farther east, reaching the farthest parts of the earth. I crossed the Red Sea and traveled far beyond it. As I continued, I passed through a region of complete darkness and kept moving forward.

Eventually, I came near the paradise of righteousness. From a distance, I saw trees larger and more numerous than any I had seen before. These trees were different—massive, beautiful, and majestic. Among them stood a special tree, the tree of wisdom. Its fruit was eaten by the holy ones to gain great knowledge. The tree was as tall as a fir tree, with leaves similar to those of a carob tree. Its fruit grew in clusters like grapes, spreading a pleasant fragrance far and wide.

I said, "This tree is so beautiful! It looks so pleasing."

Then Gabriel, the holy angel with me, said, "This is the tree of wisdom. Long ago, your first father and mother ate from it. When they did, they gained knowledge, their eyes were opened, and they realized they were naked. Because of this, they were sent out of the garden."

To The Ends of The Earth

I continued my journey to the farthest edges of the earth, where I saw enormous creatures, each one different from the others. I also saw many kinds of birds, each with its own unique shape, beauty, and voice. No two were alike.

To the east of these creatures, I reached the very edge of the earth, where the sky touches the land and the gates of heaven open. I watched as the stars appeared, coming forth through these gates. I counted each one and carefully recorded their numbers, names, positions, movements, and the times and months when they appeared, just as Uriel, the holy angel guiding me, had taught me.

He explained everything in detail, writing down their names, the times they were meant to shine, and the purpose they were created to fulfill.

Enoch's Journeys
North, West, South, And East

A Summary

I continued my journey to the north, reaching the farthest edges of the earth, where I saw incredible and amazing sights. At the very edge, I saw three gates in the sky, standing open. From these gates, the northern winds blew out. Some winds brought cold air, hail, frost, snow, dew, and rain. One of the gates released winds that were gentle and beneficial, but the other two sent out powerful winds that caused storms and hardship on the earth.

From there, I traveled west, to the farthest part of the earth, where I saw three more heavenly gates, just like the ones in the east. They had the same number of openings and let out the same kinds of winds.

Then I journeyed south, to the ends of the earth, where I saw three more heavenly gates. From these gates, the southern winds blew, carrying dew and rain.

Finally, I traveled east, reaching the farthest part of the world. There, I saw three more heavenly gates, but above them were smaller openings. Through these smaller gates, the stars of heaven passed as they moved westward, following their set paths in the sky.

After witnessing all these things, I praised—and will always praise—the Lord of glory, who created such wonderful and powerful works. He has shown His mighty deeds to His angels and to the spirits of humanity, so they may recognize His power, honor His creation, and bless Him forever.

The Book of Giants

Introduction

The mysterious figure of Enoch, briefly mentioned in the Book of Genesis, has fascinated scholars and religious thinkers for centuries. The Bible describes him as a man who "walked with God" and was taken by Him (Genesis 5:24), which has inspired many writings that explore his life and the mysteries surrounding him. One of these texts, The Book of Giants, gives a deeper look into the world before the Great Flood, focusing on events involving powerful beings known as the Watchers.

The journey of The Book of Giants from being almost unknown to gaining scholarly attention shows how ancient stories can survive over time. Pieces of this text were first discovered among the Dead Sea Scrolls in the mid-20th century, specifically in caves 1, 2, 4, and 6 at Qumran. These Aramaic fragments, written before the 2nd century BCE, helped connect the short biblical mentions of Enoch with the more detailed stories found in other ancient writings. The discovery highlighted the text's importance in understanding the religious and cultural world of the Second Temple period.

The Book of Giants tells the story of what happened when the "sons of God" came to Earth. These heavenly beings, called the Watchers, formed forbidden relationships with human women, which led to the birth of giant hybrid children known as the Nephilim. These giants, blessed with incredible strength and size, soon became violent rulers, bringing chaos and destruction to the world. The story focuses on two of these giants, Ohyah and Hahyah, the sons of the leader of the Watchers, Shemihaza. Their dreams, later explained by Enoch, warn of a coming disaster as punishment for their actions. The book highlights themes of divine justice and the dangers of breaking the natural order.

Many of the ideas in The Book of Giants are similar to stories from other ancient cultures, especially myths about gods or divine beings having children with humans. The presence of names like Gilgamesh, a well-known figure from Mesopotamian legends, suggests that the book combines elements from different traditions, showing a shared cultural history. The text also adds more details to the biblical story of the Great Flood, explaining that it was not just caused by human evil but also by the chaos created by the Watchers and their children.

Although The Book of Giants was written before the 2nd century BCE, it was kept alive through the Manichaean religion. Manichaeism, a gnostic faith that began in the 3rd century CE, adopted and modified the story, making it part of their religious teachings. Fragments of the book have been found in Turfan, Western China, proving that it was shared across many cultures and remained influential for centuries.

Today, The Book of Giants gives scholars and history enthusiasts a better understanding of early Jewish beliefs, ancient religious writings, and the development of ideas about angels and demons. The stories in this book challenge readers to think about the divide between the human and divine worlds—and what happens when those boundaries are crossed. As we explore this translation, we have the opportunity to reflect on these ancient ideas and what they say about morality, justice, and the human experience.

This version of The Book of Giants aims to stay true to its original meaning while making it easy to read and understand. It keeps the richness of the original text while helping readers see the historical and cultural background that shaped its creation.

Book of Giants -- Reconstructed Texts

A group of fallen angels came down to Earth, bringing both secret knowledge and destruction.

They learned things they were never supposed to know.

Sin spread everywhere.

They became violent and killed many people.

Their children grew into giants.

The angels used Earth's resources for themselves.

They took everything the land produced.

They ruled over the sea, the sky, and all living things.

They ate the fruit, grain, and trees.

They took animals, from wild beasts to tiny creatures, and watched everything happening on Earth.

They joined in terrible acts, bringing corruption to humanity.

The two hundred fallen angels began experimenting with different creatures, including humans.

They took donkeys, rams, goats, and other animals from the land and sky.

They used them in unnatural ways, mixing them in ways that were never meant to happen.

This corruption led to chaos, violence, and monsters roaming the Earth.

They ruined the world.

They created giants and unnatural creatures.

Their evil spread everywhere.

The Earth was filled with bloodshed, and the giants were never satisfied.

They destroyed everything and devoured whatever they could.

Monsters attacked whatever stood in their way.

The land was torn apart.

Terrifying creatures appeared and grew stronger.

They didn't understand the full impact of their actions.

Their choices made the Earth worse.

The fallen angels' influence caused great destruction.

In the end, everything would collapse because of them.

Yet, even after all this, they were never satisfied.

The giants began having strange dreams and visions. One of them, Mahway, the son of the angel Barakel, had a dream that disturbed him. He saw a tablet placed in water. When it was pulled out, only three names remained while the rest had disappeared. This seemed to warn that almost everyone would be wiped out, leaving only a few survivors—Noah and his family—after a great flood.

A tablet was soaked in water.

The water rose and covered it.

When it was lifted out, most of the names were gone.

Mahway told the other giants about his dream, and they tried to understand what it meant.

He realized the vision was a warning of disaster.

He admitted his fear to the others and spoke of the spirits of the dead, who cried out for justice against those who had killed them.

He saw that they would all die soon, and their time was almost up.

Ohya, one of the giants, asked Mahway who had given him this vision.

Mahway said his father, Barakel, had been with him.

Before he could finish, Ohya interrupted, shocked by what he had heard.

He shouted, "This is unbelievable! If even a woman who cannot have children gives birth, then something truly impossible is happening."

Ohya spoke to Hahya, saying that destruction was coming to the Earth.

When they realized this, they cried before the giants.

Ohya then told Hahya that it was not their fault, but Azaiel's.

He said the giants were the children of fallen angels, and they would not let their loved ones be abandoned.

He also said they had not been completely defeated, and they still had strength left.

The giants began to understand that they could not win against the powers of Heaven. One of the speakers might have been Gilgamesh.

A giant declared that he was strong, with great power in his arms.

He had fought against mortals and waged war, but he now realized he could not defeat his enemies.

They lived in Heaven, in sacred places, and were far stronger than him.

He had been called a wild beast and a wild man.

Then Ohya spoke and said he had a dream that disturbed him.

It kept him awake and forced him to see a vision.

He now understood something important.

His vision was about a tree being uprooted, except for three roots.

It carried the same message as a previous dream.

As he watched, three roots remained.

Then something moved them into a garden.

Ohya tried to ignore what the vision meant.

At first, he claimed it only referred to the demon Azazel.

Now, he suggested it was only about the rulers of the Earth.

The vision spoke about the fate of their souls.

Ohya told the giants what Gilgamesh had said.

The leader had cursed the rulers, and the giants were pleased by his words.

Then he left.

The giants were troubled by more dreams.

Two of them woke up, frightened by what they had seen.

They went to their fellow giants and described their visions.

One of them had dreamed of a garden.

Gardeners were watering trees.

Two hundred trees had large branches growing from their roots.

Then, fire spread and burned the entire garden.

The dreamers went to the giants and told them what they had
seen.

Someone suggested they should find Enoch to explain the
meaning of the dreams.

Ohya spoke to the giants and told them about his own dream.

He had seen the Ruler of Heaven come down to Earth.

When he finished, the giants and monsters became terrified.

They called Mahway and asked him to go find Enoch.

Mahway was sent to find Enoch, the wise scribe, to ask him about
the visions.

He flew through the air like strong winds, moving like an eagle.

He left the land behind and passed through a great desert.

When Enoch saw Mahway, he greeted him.

Mahway told him the giants and monsters were waiting for
answers.

They wanted to know what their dreams meant.

Enoch sent back a tablet with a warning.

The message was written in his own hand and was addressed to
Shemihaza and his followers.

He warned them about the things they had done.

Their wives and children had followed their wicked ways.

The land itself was crying out against them.

Because of their actions, destruction was coming.

A great flood would wipe out all life on land and sea.

But there was still a chance to change.

They were told to break free from evil and pray.

In another vision, Enoch saw something that filled him with fear.

Translated by Tim Zengerink

He collapsed to the ground when he heard a voice.

He saw a being who lived among humans but had not learned from them.

The Testament of Amram

Introduction

Among the ancient writings found in Cave 4 at Qumran, researchers uncovered a damaged Aramaic document that gives a different view of Amram, the father of Moses. This text, known as the Visions of Amram, tells a story that does not completely match the one in the Bible. It blends historical events with supernatural experiences. While it has some similarities to the Book of Exodus, it seems to be more of a unique interpretation rather than a direct account of biblical history.

One of the most interesting parts of the text is the mention of Amram's age when he died—137 years—just like it is written in Exodus 6:20. The document also gives a different timeline for how long the Israelites lived in Egypt, saying they were there for 152 years. This is much shorter than the 400 or 430 years mentioned in Genesis 15:13 and Exodus 12:40. Some experts, including J. Heinemann, have studied this shorter timeline and connected it to the idea that the Israelites were in Egypt for 210 years (JJS 22, 1971).

Experts who have studied the handwriting believe that different copies of the text were written between the second and first centuries BCE. The fragments, labeled 4Q543–549, show variations in script style, which helps estimate their age.

One of the most mysterious parts of the text describes a vision Amram had. In it, he meets two powerful supernatural beings: the Angel of Darkness, called Melkiresha, and the leader of the Army of Light. The name of this second figure is missing due to damage in the manuscript, but many scholars believe it could be Melchizedek, a mysterious priest-king mentioned in both biblical and other ancient writings.

The Testament of Amram

This is a copy of the book containing the words from the vision of Amram, son of Kehat and grandson of Levi. It includes everything he told his sons and the instructions he gave them on the day he died, at the age of 137. This was also the 152nd year since the Israelites had been exiled in Egypt.

Amram called for Uzziel, his youngest brother, and arranged for him to marry his daughter, Miriam. He told Miriam, "You are thirty years old." To celebrate, he held a feast that lasted seven days. During this time, he ate, drank, and rejoiced. When the feast was over, he sent for his son Aaron, who was about twenty years old, and told him, "Go, my son, and call the messengers, your brothers, from the house of ..."

Qahat went to live and settle in a new place, working alongside many of his relatives. Their work was difficult and continued until they had buried the dead.

In the first year of my journey, I heard troubling news about an upcoming war. With my approval, our group returned to Egypt, and I went to bury the dead. However, they did not build the tombs of our ancestors. My father, Qahat, and my wife, Jochebed, left me behind to continue working, providing them with everything they needed from the land of Canaan. We stayed in Hebron while we built.

A war broke out between the Philistines and the Egyptians. The Philistines and Canaanites defeated Egypt and blocked its borders. Because of this, my wife Jochebed was unable to leave Egypt and travel to Canaan for forty-one years. We could not return to Egypt either. The war between Egypt, Canaan, and the Philistines prevented us from being together.

During all this time, my wife remained in Egypt, separated from me. I did not take another wife. Other women were available, but I refused, hoping to return to Egypt and see my wife again in peace.

One night, I had a vision in a dream. I saw two powerful beings arguing about me. They were having a heated debate over me, so I asked them, "Why are you arguing about me?"

They replied, "We have been given control over all humans." Then they asked me, "Which one of us do you choose?"

I looked up and saw one of them. His appearance was terrifying, like a viper. His clothes were made of many colors, and his skin was extremely dark.

Then I looked at the other one. His face also resembled a snake, possibly an adder. He was covered with something strange, and over his eyes, there was...

Fr. 2

I asked about the Watcher, "Who is he?"

The other one answered, "This Watcher has three names: Belial, Prince of Darkness, and Melkiresha."

Then I asked, "My lord, what power does he have?"

He replied, "All his ways are filled with darkness, and everything he does is evil. He exists in the shadows, and he controls all that is dark. But I rule over all that is light and everything that belongs to it..."

This is a copy of the written words from the vision of Amram, son of Qahat and grandson of Levi. It contains everything he told his sons on the day he died, in the year of his death at the age of 136. This was also the 152nd year since the Israelites had been exiled in Egypt.

During this time, Amram called for his younger brother, Uzziel, and gave him Miriam, his daughter, in marriage. Miriam was thirty years old. To celebrate, he held a wedding feast that lasted seven days. He ate, drank, and rejoiced throughout the celebration. When the feast ended, he sent for his son Aaron, who was about twenty years old, and told him, "My son, call the messengers, your brothers, from the house of …"

Amram then spoke and said, "I will explain to you the meaning of your names, just as he wrote for Moses. I will also reveal the mystery of Aaron's service to God. He is a holy priest of the Most High, and all his descendants will remain holy for all generations to come. He will be known as the seventh among the men chosen by God. He will be called by this title and will be chosen as a priest forever…"

I am telling you the true path. I will share this knowledge with you.

All the Sons of Light will shine, while the Sons of Darkness will remain in darkness. The Sons of Light will grow in wisdom and understanding, but the Sons of Darkness will lose their way. In the end, the Sons of Darkness will be removed.

Fools and wicked people will live in darkness, but those who are wise and righteous will shine. The Sons of Light will move toward the light, while the Sons of Darkness will face death and destruction.

The people will be surrounded by brightness, and they will be taught the truth.

The Dream Visions

Chapter LXXXII

Now, my son Methuselah, I will tell you about all the visions I have seen, explaining them to you in full detail.

Before I got married, I had two visions, and each one was very different from the other. The first vision came to me while I was learning to write, and the second happened just before I married your mother. The second vision was frightening, and I prayed to the Lord about both of them.

One night, I was resting in my grandfather Mahalalel's house when I suddenly had a vision. In it, I saw the sky collapse and fall as if it had been torn away and brought down to the earth. As the heavens fell, the earth was swallowed up by a huge abyss. I watched as mighty mountains crumbled on top of each other, and hills sank down, piling onto other hills. The tallest trees were ripped from the ground, torn apart, and thrown into the abyss, disappearing into the darkness.

As I watched this terrible destruction, words poured out of my mouth, and I cried out loudly, "The earth is being destroyed!"

My grandfather Mahalalel woke me up and asked, "Why are you crying out like this, my son? Why are you so troubled?"

I told him everything I had seen in my vision, describing it in detail. After listening, Mahalalel said to me, "What you have seen is truly terrible, my son. Your dream has great meaning, for it reveals the truth about the sins of the world. The earth will fall into ruin and be destroyed in a great disaster.

"Now, my son, get up and pray to the Lord of glory. Because you are faithful, ask Him to allow some people to survive, so that He does not completely destroy everything."

He continued, "What you saw will come down from the heavens upon the earth. A great disaster is coming, and nothing will escape."

Following his advice, I got up and prayed with all my heart. I begged the Lord to have mercy, writing down my prayer so that future generations could understand what was coming. Now, I am sharing all of this with you, my son Methuselah.

Later, when I went outside, I looked up at the sky. I saw the sun rising in the east, the moon setting in the west, and a few stars shining above. As I looked around at the earth and everything in it, I saw how perfectly everything still followed the order God had set from the beginning.

I praised the Lord, the Judge of all things, and thanked Him for His wisdom and power. I gave thanks that He made the sun rise in the east, move across the sky, and follow the path it had been given since the beginning of time.

Chapter LXXXIII

I raised my hands in righteousness and praised the Holy and Great One. With the breath in my lungs and the tongue that God has given to people, I spoke. God created this tongue and breath so that humans could speak, express their thoughts, and offer prayers.

"Blessed are You, O Lord, the Mighty King. You are great and powerful, the ruler of all creation in heaven. You are the King of kings and the God of the whole world. Your power, authority, and greatness will last forever. Through every generation, Your rule remains the same. The heavens are Your eternal throne, and the earth is like a footstool beneath You, firmly established forever.

You have made everything and have control over all things—nothing is beyond Your power. Wisdom is always with You and never leaves Your side. You know everything, You see everything, and You hear everything. Nothing is hidden from You because all things are visible before Your eyes.

But now, the angels of heaven have disobeyed, and Your anger rests upon the people of the earth until the great day of judgment.

O God, Lord, and Mighty King, I come before You, humbly asking You to hear my prayer. I beg You to allow some people to remain on the earth and not to completely wipe out all flesh, leaving the land empty. Please do not bring total destruction that leaves no one to live upon the earth.

Instead, my Lord, remove from the earth those who have brought about Your anger. Let those who live in righteousness and goodness remain, like a plant that grows and spreads forever. Please, Lord, hear my prayer and do not turn away from my request."

Chapter LXXXIV

After this, I had another dream, and now, my son, I will tell you everything I saw.

Enoch spoke to his son Methuselah, saying, "Listen carefully to me, my son. Pay close attention to this dream-vision that I, your father, have seen.

Before I married your mother, Edna, I had a vision while lying in bed. In my dream, I saw a white bull rise from the earth. Then a heifer appeared, and with her came two more bulls—one was black, and the other was red.

The black bull attacked the red bull, striking him with its horns and chasing him across the land. After that, I could no longer see the red bull because he had disappeared.

The black bull grew larger, and the heifer stayed by his side. Then I saw many oxen come from the black bull. They looked like him and followed his lead.

The first cow—the one that had appeared earlier—left the first white bull to search for the red bull. She could not find him, and she cried out in sadness, mourning him as she searched.

Then the first white bull came to her and comforted her. After that, she stopped crying.

Later, she gave birth to another white bull. Afterward, she had many more bulls and black cows.

In my dream, I saw that the white bull also grew, becoming a great and powerful bull. From him came many more white bulls, and they all looked like him. These white bulls began to multiply, producing even more white bulls generation after generation, growing in number.

Chapter LXXXV

As I continued dreaming, I saw another vision with my own eyes. I looked up at the sky, and suddenly, I saw a star fall from the heavens. It landed among the oxen and started to live and feed among them.

Then I saw a large group of black oxen. To my surprise, they all left their usual fields and pastures and gathered in one place. They mixed together, blending their herds.

Again, I looked up at the sky in my vision, and I saw many more stars coming down. They joined the first star and also became bulls among the oxen. These new bulls lived and grazed among the cattle as if they belonged there.

As I watched, I noticed something strange. These bulls extended their private parts, like horses do, and began mating with the cows in the herd. The cows became pregnant and gave birth to unusual animals—elephants, camels, and donkeys.

The oxen were terrified of these strange creatures. They were afraid and started to fight back. They bit them, gored them with their horns, and tried to defend themselves.

But the creatures did not stop. They fought back against the oxen, attacking and devouring them. Chaos broke out, and all the people on earth were filled with fear. They trembled in terror and started running, trying to escape from the destruction caused by these powerful creatures.

Chapter LXXXVI

I continued watching as the creatures turned on each other, attacking and devouring one another. They fought violently, goring each other with their horns. The earth itself seemed to cry out because of all the chaos and destruction.

Then I looked up to the sky and saw another vision. I saw beings coming down from heaven, and they looked like men dressed in white robes. Four of them arrived first, followed by three more.

The last three came directly to me. They took my hand and lifted me up, carrying me away from the people on earth. They brought me to a high place, far above the ground, where I could see everything happening below. From there, they showed me a massive tower that stretched so high into the sky that even the surrounding hills looked small beside it.

One of them spoke to me and said, "Stay here and watch carefully. Pay close attention to everything that happens to the elephants, camels, donkeys, stars, and oxen. Observe them all."

Chapter LXXXVII

I saw one of the four beings who had arrived first. He grabbed the first star that had fallen from the sky, tied its hands and feet, and threw it into a deep, dark abyss. The abyss was narrow and terrifying, filled with shadows.

Then one of the beings pulled out a sword and gave it to the elephants, camels, and donkeys. They immediately began attacking each other, striking with great force. The earth shook beneath them because of their violent battle.

As I kept watching, I saw one of the four beings throw large stones down from the sky onto them. He then gathered all the great stars—the ones whose bodies looked like horses—and tied their hands and feet. After binding them, he threw them deep into the abyss beneath the earth.

Chapter LXXXVIII

One of the four beings went to the white bull and secretly taught him something without scaring him. Although the bull was born as an animal, he changed into a man and built a large vessel for himself. He lived inside the vessel, and three other bulls joined him. They all remained safely inside.

Then I looked up and saw a high roof with seven streams of water pouring down from it. The water flowed heavily into a large enclosure.

As I watched, fountains opened from the ground, and the water started rising higher and higher. It grew until it completely covered everything inside the enclosure.

The water, along with darkness and mist, continued to rise. It overflowed the enclosure and spread across the earth.

All the animals inside the enclosure were gathered together, but they sank into the deep water. They were swallowed by the flood and drowned.

But the vessel floated safely on the surface of the water. Meanwhile, the oxen, elephants, camels, donkeys, and all the other animals were lost beneath the waves. I could no longer see them as they disappeared into the depths.

Then, I saw the water begin to drain away from the high roof. The deep cracks in the earth were filled, and new abysses opened up. The water flowed into these abysses until the land became visible again. The vessel came to rest on solid ground, the darkness faded, and light returned.

The white bull, who had become a man, stepped out of the vessel along with the three bulls that had been inside with him. One of them was white like him, another was red like blood, and the third was black. Then the white bull left the others.

From that moment, they began to bring forth different animals and birds. There were lions, tigers, wolves, dogs, hyenas, wild boars, foxes, squirrels, pigs, falcons, vultures, kites, eagles, and ravens. Among them, a white bull was born.

But the animals started attacking and biting each other. The white bull that was born fathered a wild donkey and another white bull. The wild donkeys began to multiply.

The bull that came from him had a black wild boar and a white sheep. The wild boar produced many more boars, while the sheep gave birth to twelve sheep.

When the twelve sheep grew up, one of them was given to the donkeys. The donkeys then handed that sheep over to the wolves, and the sheep lived among the wolves as it matured.

Then the Lord brought the remaining eleven sheep to be with the one that had been given to the wolves. They stayed together among the wolves and their numbers increased.

The wolves started fearing the growing flocks of sheep. To stop them, the wolves attacked the sheep, harming them and killing their young. They even threw the lambs into a great river. The sheep cried out in distress for their lost young and pleaded with their Lord for help.

One sheep managed to escape from the wolves and ran to the wild donkeys. I saw the sheep crying out, begging its Lord with all its strength. Their cries reached the Lord, who came down from His high place to rescue and care for the sheep.

The Lord called the sheep that had escaped from the wolves and told it to go back and warn the wolves not to harm the sheep anymore.

The sheep obeyed and went to the wolves, just as the Lord had instructed. Along the way, another sheep joined it. Together, the two sheep entered the gathering of wolves and gave them the Lord's warning.

But the wolves did not listen. They continued attacking and mistreating the sheep with all their strength. The sheep cried out loudly for help.

Then the Lord came to protect the sheep, and the sheep began to fight back against the wolves. The wolves cried and wailed, but the sheep became calm and stopped calling out.

I watched as the sheep left the presence of the wolves. However, the wolves were blinded and could no longer see clearly. Even so, they still chased after the sheep with all their might.

The Lord of the sheep walked with them as their leader, and all the sheep followed Him. His presence was bright, glorious, and powerful.

The wolves kept chasing the sheep until they reached a great sea. Suddenly, the sea split, and the water stood like walls on both sides, creating a dry path for the sheep. The Lord of the sheep led them safely through, standing between them and the wolves.

The wolves, still unable to see clearly, followed the sheep into the sea. But when they finally saw the Lord of the sheep, they turned and tried to run away. At that moment, the sea returned to normal. The waters rushed back together and covered the wolves completely.

I watched until all the wolves that had chased the sheep were drowned.

The sheep made it safely out of the water and entered a wilderness. The land was dry, with no water or grass, but the sheep's eyes were opened, and they could finally see clearly. I saw the Lord of the sheep taking care of them, giving them water and food to keep them strong. One sheep stepped forward and became their guide.

That sheep climbed to the top of a tall rock, and the Lord of the sheep sent it back to lead the others.

Then I saw the Lord of the sheep standing in front of them. His appearance was great and powerful. All the sheep looked at Him in awe and fear.

They trembled and said to the sheep leading them, "We cannot stand before our Lord or even look at Him."

The leading sheep returned to the top of the rock, but the other sheep began to lose their way. They became blind again and wandered off the path the leader had shown them. The leader did not notice this at first.

The Lord of the sheep became very angry with them. When the leader finally realized what had happened, it came down from the rock and went to the lost sheep. Many of them had strayed far from the flock and could no longer see.

When the lost sheep saw the leader coming, they became afraid and trembled. They wanted to return to the flock.

The leader took some of the other sheep and went to find the lost ones. It disciplined those who had wandered away, and the sheep were afraid of it. Through this, the leader was able to bring the lost sheep back, and they returned safely to their flock.

In my vision, I saw that one of the sheep changed into a man and built a house for the Lord of the sheep. He gathered all the sheep and brought them into the house so they could live there.

I kept watching until the sheep that had met the leader fell asleep. Then I saw that all the great sheep passed away, and younger sheep took their place. These smaller sheep moved to a pasture and came near a flowing stream of water.

The sheep that had become a man, their leader, stepped away from them and also fell asleep. The rest of the sheep searched for him and cried out in sadness.

After a while, they stopped mourning for him and crossed the stream. Two new sheep rose up as leaders to guide them in place of the ones who had fallen asleep.

The sheep arrived in a beautiful and peaceful land, a wonderful place where they had everything they needed. In this land, the house of the Lord stood among them.

Sometimes their eyes were open, and they could see clearly, but at other times, they became blind again. Another sheep came and led them back to the right path, helping them see once more.

Then dogs, foxes, and wild boars came and attacked the sheep, killing many of them. The Lord of the sheep raised up a strong ram from among the flock to lead and protect them.

The ram fought back against the dogs, foxes, and wild boars, striking them down and pushing them away.

The sheep whose eyes had been opened saw the ram among them. But the ram turned away from its position of honor. Instead of protecting the sheep, it began to harm them, trampling on them and treating them unfairly.

So the Lord of the sheep sent a lamb to another lamb and raised it up to become a new ram, a new leader to take the place of the one who had abandoned his duty.

The Lord spoke privately to this new ram, making him a prince and a leader for the sheep. But during this time, the dogs continued to attack and oppress the flock.

The first ram turned against the second ram, chasing it, and the second ram fled. Then I saw the dogs drag down the first ram.

The second ram stood up and led the young sheep. The sheep multiplied and grew in number. The dogs, foxes, and wild boars became afraid and ran away from the new ram. This ram fought against the wild animals, striking them down, and they no longer had any power over the sheep. They could no longer steal or hurt them.

The ram had many offspring, but eventually, it fell asleep. A young sheep rose in its place, becoming the new ram, the new prince, and leader of the flock.

The house of the Lord became bigger and stronger to hold all the sheep. A tall and magnificent tower was built on top of the house for the Lord of the sheep. Even though the house itself was simple, the tower was grand and impressive. The Lord of the sheep stood at the top of the tower, and the sheep gathered to offer Him a feast.

But once again, the sheep strayed from the right path. They wandered in different directions and abandoned the house of the Lord. The Lord sent some sheep to call them back, but the flock turned against them and killed them.

One sheep survived and escaped. It cried out over the flock, warning them, but the other sheep tried to kill it too. The Lord of the sheep saved this one, bringing it to a safe place to live with Him.

The Lord sent many more sheep to warn the flock and call them back, but they refused to listen. These messengers mourned over the sheep's disobedience.

Then I saw that the sheep completely abandoned the Lord's house and His tower. They became blind again. The Lord of the sheep brought great judgment upon them. He struck down many of them because they had turned away, bringing destruction upon themselves and betraying His holy place.

He handed them over to lions, tigers, wolves, hyenas, foxes, and all kinds of wild beasts. These animals attacked the sheep, tearing them apart and eating them piece by piece.

I saw that He allowed their house and tower to be destroyed, giving them over to the lions and wild animals to be torn apart completely. The destruction was total.

I cried out as loudly as I could, begging the Lord of the sheep to stop this. I told Him what was happening to them and pleaded with Him to save them from being devoured by the wild beasts.

But He did not answer. Instead, He let the beasts continue attacking and stealing from the sheep. He allowed them to be destroyed, and He did not step in to stop it.

Then He called seventy shepherds and put them in charge of the sheep. He spoke to these shepherds and their helpers, saying, "From now on, each of you will care for the sheep. You must follow every command I give you and obey all My instructions."

"I will count the sheep and give them to you. I will tell you which ones should be destroyed, and you must destroy only the ones I command."

Then He gave the sheep to their care and assigned another being to watch over them. He told the observer, "Pay close attention to what the shepherds do. Write down everything they destroy. They will destroy far more than I have ordered.

"Keep a record of every act of destruction. Note how many are destroyed by My command and how many are destroyed by their own choice. Write down the actions of each shepherd and how much damage they cause.

"When the time comes, bring Me the records, showing how many sheep they destroyed and how many they gave over to be destroyed. This will be proof against them, so I will know whether they obeyed or disobeyed My instructions.

"Do not warn the shepherds or tell them what you are doing. Just write down everything they do in their time and present it to Me."

I watched as the shepherds took care of the sheep during their appointed times. But they began to kill and destroy far more than they were told. They handed the sheep over to the lions and other wild animals.

The lions, tigers, and wild boars ate most of the sheep. They also burned down the tower and destroyed the house where the sheep lived.

I was heartbroken when I saw the destruction of the tower and the house. After that, I could no longer tell if the sheep ever returned to it.

The shepherds and their helpers continued giving the sheep to wild animals to be devoured. Each shepherd had a set time to act, and the observer recorded everything. He wrote down how many sheep each shepherd destroyed.

Every shepherd killed far more than they were told to. I wept as I watched so many sheep being destroyed.

In my vision, I saw the observer writing down every act of destruction the shepherds committed, keeping a daily record. Then he took the book of records and presented it to the Lord of the sheep. He showed the Lord everything the shepherds had done, including how many sheep they had killed or given over to destruction.

The Lord took the book, read it, sealed it, and placed it beside Him.

I saw the shepherds continue their work for a while. Then three sheep returned and started rebuilding the house that had been destroyed. They also worked to restore the tower, even though wild boars tried to stop them. But the boars failed.

The sheep successfully rebuilt the house and restored the tower, naming it the High Tower. They placed a table before the tower, but the bread on the table was impure and unclean.

Through all of this, the sheep were blind and unable to see the truth, as were their shepherds. Large numbers of sheep were given to the shepherds to be destroyed. The shepherds trampled on the sheep and devoured them.

The Lord of the sheep did not interfere, allowing the sheep to be scattered across the fields and mixed with wild animals. The shepherds did nothing to protect them from the beasts.

The observer who had recorded everything brought the book back to the Lord. He read from it and pleaded for the sheep, asking the Lord to have mercy on them. He presented all the shepherds' actions as evidence. The Lord took the book, placed it beside Him, and the observer left.

Chapter LXXXIX

I kept watching as thirty-five shepherds took turns caring for the sheep. Each one completed their time, just like the shepherds before them. When one finished, the sheep were passed to the next, and each did their job during their appointed time.

Then, in my vision, I saw birds from the sky swoop down upon the sheep. Eagles led them, followed by vultures, kites, and ravens. Together, they attacked the sheep, tearing at their flesh and pecking out their eyes.

The sheep cried out in pain, but the birds kept attacking, ripping them apart. I felt deep sorrow as I watched this happen. The shepherds were supposed to protect the sheep, but they did nothing to help.

The birds kept attacking until nothing was left of the sheep—no flesh, no skin, not even tendons, only their bones scattered on the ground. Over time, even the bones disappeared, and the number of sheep grew very small.

As time passed, twenty-three more shepherds took turns caring for the sheep. They each served their time, covering fifty-eight periods.

Despite everything, new lambs were born among the white sheep. These young ones opened their eyes and began to see. They cried out for help, but the older sheep didn't listen. Their ears had grown dull, and their eyes were completely blind.

Then, I saw ravens swoop down and attack the lambs. One lamb was captured, torn apart, and eaten. But then, I noticed that some of the lambs began to grow small horns. The ravens tried to break them off. However, one of the sheep grew a large, strong horn, and its eyes were fully opened.

This sheep looked around, and as it did, the other sheep also began to open their eyes. It cried out loudly, and the rams gathered around it. But the eagles, vultures, ravens, and kites kept attacking the sheep, tearing and devouring them. The sheep stayed silent in their pain, but the rams wept and cried out in distress.

The ravens then focused on the sheep with the great horn. They fought fiercely against it, trying to break its horn, but they couldn't defeat it.

Then, I saw the shepherds, along with the eagles, vultures, and kites, urging the ravens to break the great horn of the ram. They all joined together to attack it. The ram fought back and cried out for help.

I kept watching until the man who had been keeping the record of the shepherds came to help the ram. He showed the ram everything that had been written down and had come to assist it.

At that moment, the Lord of the sheep appeared in His anger. Everyone who saw Him was terrified and ran, falling under the weight of His presence.

The eagles, vultures, ravens, kites, and all the sheep gathered together to try to break the ram's horn. But the man who had been keeping records opened the book before the Lord of the sheep. He showed how the last twelve shepherds had destroyed far more sheep than the ones before them.

Then, the Lord of the sheep took His staff and struck the earth. The ground split open, and all the beasts and birds that had attacked the sheep were swallowed up. Then the ground closed over them.

A great sword was given to the sheep, and they rose up against the remaining beasts, striking them down. The surviving beasts and birds fled in fear.

Then I saw a throne set up in a beautiful and peaceful land. The Lord of the sheep sat upon the throne. The man who had kept the sealed records brought them forward and opened them before the Lord of the sheep.

The Lord called upon the seven men—the first white ones—who had been with Him from the beginning. He commanded them to gather all the fallen stars, starting with the first one that had led the others astray. These stars were the ones that had taken on the appearance of horses. The seven white ones obeyed, bringing all the stars before the Lord to stand in His presence.

Then the Lord turned to the man standing among the seven white ones—the one who had been recording everything. He said, "Take those seventy shepherds to whom I entrusted the sheep. They went beyond what I commanded and destroyed far more than they should have. Bring them forward for judgment."

I saw the seventy shepherds with their hands tied. They were brought before the Lord, waiting to be judged.

The judgment started with the stars. Each one was judged and found guilty of breaking the laws given to them. As punishment, they were sent to a place of destruction. I saw them thrown into a deep, fiery pit filled with raging flames. The fire rose high, consuming everything. It was a terrifying sight—a place of complete and final punishment.

Then the seventy shepherds were judged. One by one, they were found guilty for exceeding their orders, and they too were thrown into the fiery abyss, the same place where the stars had been cast.

I saw another pit open up in the middle of the earth. Fire blazed within it, and the blind sheep were brought forward. They were judged and found guilty, then thrown into the burning abyss, one after another. This second pit was located to the right of the house.

I watched as the fire consumed them completely, even their bones were burned to ashes. The destruction was total.

Then, I saw the old house being folded up and taken away. Its pillars, beams, and decorations were all removed and placed somewhere in the south.

After that, the Lord of the sheep brought out a new house. This house was far bigger and more magnificent than the first. It was set up in the same place as the old one, but everything about it was new—its pillars, beams, and decorations. It was greater and more beautiful than before. All the sheep were gathered into this house.

I saw that the remaining sheep, along with every animal of the land and every bird of the sky, bowed before the sheep, honoring them. They obeyed the sheep in everything.

Then, the three white-robed figures who had taken me by the hand earlier appeared again. The ram that had also led me before was with them. They lifted me up and set me down in the middle of the sheep as the final judgment was about to begin.

Now, all the sheep were white, their wool thick and clean. Everything that had been lost or destroyed was restored. All the wild animals and birds were gathered together in the new house. The Lord of the sheep was filled with joy because everything had been made right again, and His house was full of goodness.

Then, I saw the sword that had been given to the sheep before. It was returned to the house and sealed there in the presence of the Lord. After this, all the sheep entered the house, though it was so large that they could not fill it completely.

The eyes of all the sheep were opened—they could all see clearly now. None were blind anymore. They looked around and saw the goodness surrounding them. The house became even larger, full of joy and life.

Then I saw a white bull born among the sheep. It had large, powerful horns, and all the animals of the land and the birds of the sky feared it. They continually made requests to it, recognizing its strength.

As time passed, I saw all the sheep transform. They became white bulls like the first. Among them, one was born as a lamb, but it grew into a strong and mighty creature. It developed large black horns on its head. The Lord of the sheep rejoiced over this lamb and all the oxen.

I lay down among them and fell asleep. When I woke up, I remembered everything I had seen in my vision. I blessed the Lord of righteousness and gave Him praise.

But I also wept deeply. Tears flowed without stopping as I thought about everything that had been revealed to me. It was overwhelming. I cried because I understood that everything I had seen would come true, and all the actions of humanity, in their proper time, had been shown to me.

That night, I remembered the very first dream I had received. Its memory came back to me, and it troubled me. I wept again, feeling the weight of the vision and all that it foretold.

Chapter XC

The book written by Enoch contains teachings of wisdom, meant to guide people in living rightly. It is a message for all my children on earth and for future generations—those who want to live in truth and peace.

Do not let your heart be troubled by the times you live in. Remember, the Holy and Great One has set specific times for everything. Every event happens according to His plan.

In those days, the righteous will awaken as if from a deep sleep. They will walk in the ways of truth and justice, living with kindness and grace.

The Lord will bless the righteous, giving them strength to live in goodness and truth. They will walk in His eternal light, never again facing darkness.

But sin will be completely destroyed. It will disappear forever, never to return. From that moment on, there will be no more sin, and it will never be remembered again.

Chapter XCI

"And now, my son Methuselah, gather your brothers and bring together all the sons of your mother. The Lord has spoken to me, and His spirit is upon me. I must share with you everything that will happen to you and your descendants for all time."

Methuselah immediately called his brothers and gathered their relatives. When they were all together, Enoch spoke to them and said:

"Listen carefully, my sons, to the words of your father. Pay close attention to what I am about to tell you. My beloved children, love what is right and always follow the path of righteousness.

Do not pretend to be righteous while hiding dishonesty in your heart. Do not follow people who are deceitful and live with divided hearts. Instead, walk in truth with sincerity. Righteousness will guide you and help you live an honest and good life.

I must tell you what I know: Violence on the earth will increase greatly. A time of punishment is coming, and all evil will be wiped out. Its foundations will be destroyed, and everything built on wickedness will crumble.

Yet, sin and evil will rise again, spreading even more than before. People will turn away from what is right. Rebellion, corruption, and dishonesty will cover the earth. Sin and wickedness will multiply, filling the world with darkness.

When this happens, punishment will come from heaven. The holy Lord, full of justice, will come to judge the world. He will punish the wicked and those who refuse to follow His ways.

In those days, violence will be completely removed. Evil and deception will be torn out and destroyed. People who worship false gods will abandon their idols, and their temples will be burned. Idolatry will be wiped out, and those who refuse to turn away from false gods will face judgment.

But the righteous will awaken. Wisdom will return to them, and they will understand what is true. They will stand in the light of the Lord and follow His ways.

Then, sin and wickedness will be cut off, and those who commit acts of violence will be destroyed. Evil will not last, and those who reject the truth will perish.

Now, my sons, I tell you this so you may clearly see the difference between righteousness and wickedness. I have shown you these things so that you may understand what is coming.

Listen to me, my sons, and always choose the path of righteousness. Do not follow the ways of violence, because all who live in wickedness will be destroyed forever."

Chapter XCII

After this, Enoch began reading from the sacred books and spoke to his sons, saying:

"I will now tell you about the children of righteousness, those chosen by God, and the seed of uprightness. My sons, I, Enoch, am sharing with you what has been revealed to me through a heavenly vision. These are truths I have learned from the holy angels and the knowledge written on the heavenly tablets."

Enoch opened the books and began to explain their contents:

"I was born in the seventh generation during the first period of time, when judgment and righteousness still ruled the earth. It was a time of balance and truth, where justice and virtue guided life.

After me, in the second period, great wickedness will spread across the earth. Deception will take root, leading people away from what is right. This time will bring the first great judgment. However, one man will be saved, kept as a sign of hope. But after this, sin will grow again, and laws will be created to suit sinners, marking a time of moral decline.

In the third period, near its end, a man will be chosen to represent righteous judgment. He will stand as a symbol of justice, and his descendants will continue the path of righteousness forever.

In the fourth period, as it nears its end, visions of holiness and righteousness will appear. A divine law will be given for future generations, and a sacred place will be created to protect and guide the faithful.

At the end of the fifth period, a house of glory and power will be built. This house will be a symbol of divine rule and will stand forever.

During the sixth period, the people living in the house of power will lose their sight, blinded by their own godlessness. They will turn away from wisdom and reject it completely. In this time of spiritual blindness, one man will rise, marking an important moment in history. But by the end of this period, the house of power will be destroyed by fire, and the chosen people will be scattered across the earth.

In the seventh period, a rebellious generation will emerge. Their actions will be many, but they will turn against righteousness. Everything they do will reflect their disobedience and rejection of the truth.

At the end of this time, the chosen ones of the eternal seed of righteousness will be selected. They will be given a sevenfold understanding of all creation, allowing them to grasp the deep mysteries of God.

Who among humanity can hear the voice of the Holy One without trembling? Who can truly understand His thoughts or comprehend all the wonders of heaven? Who can look up at the vast skies and fully grasp their wonders? Who can understand the nature of a soul or spirit, explain its mysteries, or travel to the farthest reaches of heaven to understand its purpose?

Who among men can measure the size of the earth? Who has been shown the full extent of its dimensions? Who can truly understand the height of the heavens, their vastness, their foundation, or count all the stars and the places where they rest?"

Chapter XCIII

After that, there will be another period, the eighth time, a time of righteousness. During this time, a sword will be given, representing the power to bring justice against those who oppress others. Fair judgment will be carried out, and sinners will be handed over to the righteous, who will carry out the will of God with honesty and fairness.

As this period comes to an end, those who have lived righteously will receive homes as a reward for their goodness. These homes will be places of peace and safety, built because of their faithfulness. Also, a magnificent house will be created—a house of eternal glory for the Great King, where His presence will remain forever. This house will shine brightly, showing the everlasting greatness of the Creator.

During this time, all people will be drawn to the path of righteousness. Their hearts will turn toward goodness, and they will want to follow the ways of truth and justice.

Next, in the ninth period, righteous judgment will be revealed to the whole world. Everything that was hidden will be exposed, and fairness will be made clear to all. The works of wicked people will completely disappear from the earth. Every trace of their influence and every sinful act will be gone. The earth itself will be prepared for its final purpose, as planned by God.

Then, in the tenth period, during its seventh part, the great and final judgment will take place. It will be a time of reckoning, when even the angels who have rebelled will face punishment. The Lord will bring everything into judgment, making sure that justice is fully established in both heaven and earth.

At that time, the first heaven will pass away, as it will no longer be needed, and a new heaven will take its place. This new heaven will shine brighter than ever before, as all the powers of heaven will give off a sevenfold light. This brilliant light will cover all creation, marking the complete renewal of the universe.

After this, time will continue forever without end. Everything will be filled with goodness and righteousness. Sin will be completely gone; it will never be remembered or spoken of again. The days of evil will be erased forever, and all of creation will live in perfect peace, surrounded by the everlasting light and presence of the Holy One.

Chapter XCIV

And now, my sons, I tell you to love and follow righteousness. Let it guide your choices and actions, because righteousness leads to true life and peace. But the ways of evil will come to a sudden and complete end, disappearing as if they never existed.

In every generation, some people will see the dangers of wickedness and destruction. They will understand the harm these paths bring and will choose to stay far away from them.

Now I speak to you, the righteous: Do not walk in the ways of evil or follow the path that leads to death. Stay far from it, so you do not share in its destruction. Instead, choose the path of righteousness, a way that is pure and set apart. Live a life of peace, and you will find true joy and blessings.

Remember my words and keep them in your hearts. Let them always be in your minds, and do not forget them. I know that sinners will try to lead others astray. They will tempt people to ignore wisdom, pushing it away so that no one listens to it. They will try to erase wisdom from the world, leaving nothing to protect people from falling into sin.

Trouble will come to those who build their lives on lies and cruelty. Those who use deception to carry out their plans will be destroyed. Their efforts will amount to nothing, and they will find no peace in the end.

Woe to those who build their homes on sin, using evil as their foundation. Their houses will crumble, and they will fall with them. Those who gain wealth through injustice will soon lose everything.

Woe to you who are rich, because you have put your trust in your wealth instead of in the Most High. Your riches will disappear, and you will be separated from them forever. While you lived in comfort, you forgot the Creator who gave you life. Now, everything you depended on will be taken from you.

You have spoken against God and committed many wrongs. Because of your actions, a day of judgment is coming—a day of darkness, destruction, and no escape.

So I tell you: The One who created you will bring you down. Your fall will be complete, and there will be no mercy. Your Creator will take no pleasure in you, only in your downfall, because you refused to follow His ways.

In those days, the righteous will stand as a witness against the wicked. Their lives will prove that those who rejected the truth made the wrong choice. The difference between the righteous and the sinners will be clear, and the righteous will see the judgment carried out on those who refused to follow the path of truth.

Chapter XCV

Oh, how I wish my eyes were like a cloud full of water so that I could cry for you, letting my tears fall like heavy rain. If I could do that, maybe it would ease the pain in my heart.

Who has allowed you to do such shameful and wicked things? Because of your actions, judgment is coming for you, sinners, and there will be no way to escape it.

But to the righteous, I say: Do not be afraid of sinners or their evil ways. The Lord will soon give you power over them. You will have the right to bring justice upon them and judge them as you see fit.

Trouble will come to those who speak curses that can never be taken back. Because of the weight of your sins, there will be no healing for you. You have cut yourselves off from any chance of being restored.

Trouble will come to those who treat others unfairly, repaying kindness with evil. The same harm you have done to others will come back to you, for you will be judged by your own actions.

Woe to those who lie and falsely accuse others. Woe to those who cheat and make dishonest decisions. Your punishment will come quickly, and your life will end without warning.

Woe to you sinners who hurt and mistreat the righteous. You may cause them suffering now, but soon, you will suffer too. You will be handed over for judgment because of the injustice you have done. The weight of your sins will press down on you, and there will be no escape.

Chapter XCVI

Have hope, you who live righteously, because the time is coming when sinners will suddenly disappear before you. You will rise above them and have power over them, fulfilling the desires of your heart.

Do not be afraid, you who have suffered. Healing is coming, and a bright light will shine upon you. You will hear words of comfort from heaven, bringing you peace and reassurance.

Trouble is coming for you, sinners, who pretend to be good because of your wealth. You may look righteous on the outside, but your hearts tell the truth—you are guilty. This truth will stand as evidence against you, proving your wrongdoing.

Trouble is coming for those who feast on the finest food and drink wine in excess while using their power to crush the weak. Your greed and cruelty will not go unpunished.

Trouble is coming for those who chase after every pleasure, searching for satisfaction but never finding it. You will be taken away suddenly and disappear because you turned away from the true source of life.

Trouble is coming for those who live in dishonesty, corruption, and disrespect toward the Lord. Your actions will be remembered as a lasting record against you.

Trouble is coming for the strong who use their power to mistreat the innocent. Your destruction is near, and no amount of strength will save you from judgment.

In those days, the righteous will finally see many good and joyful days. They will live in peace and fairness, even as judgment falls upon the wicked.

Chapter XCVII

You who live righteously, be confident in this: sinners will be put to shame and destroyed. On the day of judgment, all evil will be completely erased.

You sinners, understand this: the Most High has not forgotten what you have done, and He will not ignore your downfall. The angels in heaven will celebrate when your time of judgment comes because justice will finally be served.

What will you do then, sinners? Where will you run when the prayers of the righteous reach the Lord's ears on that great day? There will be no escape. You will share the fate of those who are condemned, and this truth will stand against you: "You followed the ways of sinners and chose to live like them."

On that day, the prayers of the righteous will rise to the Lord like a sweet perfume, and your judgment will come. Every lie, every act of deceit, and every evil thing you have done will be read aloud before the Great Holy One. Your faces will burn with shame as your actions are exposed, and He will reject all your works because they were built on wickedness.

Trouble is coming for you, sinners, whether you live on land or at sea. Even the memory of you will serve as proof of your wrongdoing.

Trouble is coming for those who have collected silver and gold through dishonest ways and proudly say, "We are rich! We have gained everything we wanted. We own great wealth, have achieved all our goals, and have hired many workers. Our storehouses are overflowing like they are filled with water."

But know this: your lies will disappear like rushing water, gone as quickly as they came. Your wealth will not last or remain with you. Instead, it will rise and vanish, leaving you with nothing because you gained it dishonestly. Because of this, a great curse will fall upon you, and all your riches will lead to your destruction.

Chapter XCVIII

I promise you, both the wise and the foolish, that you will experience many things on this earth.

People will try to make themselves look more impressive than others. Men will dress even more extravagantly than young women, wearing bright, fancy clothes meant for royalty. They will cover themselves in gold, silver, and purple robes, throwing lavish parties and wasting their riches like water.

But because of this excess, they will lack true wisdom. Their pride will lead to their downfall, and they will lose everything along with their lives. Their wealth and fame will disappear, leaving them ashamed, ruined, and helpless. Their spirits will be thrown into a fire with no escape.

I promise you, sinners, that just as mountains are not made to be slaves and hills do not serve women, sin was not placed on the earth by force. Instead, people have created sin for themselves. Those who choose to sin will bring a curse upon themselves that will last forever.

Likewise, women were not created to be barren, but some die without children because of their own choices. Their actions determine their fate.

I swear to you by the Holy and Great One that all your wicked deeds are known and recorded in heaven. Nothing you do is hidden—

every act of oppression is seen by the Most High.

Do not fool yourselves into thinking that your sins are secret or unnoticed. Every single wrong you commit is written down in heaven each day, waiting for the time of judgment.

Trouble is coming for you who are foolish, because your own foolishness will destroy you. You fight against those who are wise, and because of that, nothing good will come to you.

Know this: you are being prepared for the day of destruction. Sinners, do not expect to live long lives. You will leave this world and die, with no way to escape the final judgment. There will be no one to save you when that day comes, only suffering and shame for your souls.

Trouble is coming for those of you who have stubborn hearts, who do evil, and who spill innocent blood. How can you expect to enjoy food and drink, the good things in life, when you have taken them by force? These blessings were given by the Lord, the Most High, for everyone. But because of your wickedness, you will have no peace.

Trouble is coming for those who take pleasure in sin. Why do you think good things will come to you? The righteous will be given power over you, and they will carry out judgment without mercy.

Trouble is coming for those who celebrate when the righteous suffer. No one will prepare a grave for you when you die.

Trouble is coming for those who ignore the words of the righteous. You will have no hope of life.

Trouble is coming for those who write lies and wicked words. You deceive others and lead them to harm their neighbors.

Because of your actions, you will never find peace. Your end will come suddenly, and you will face death without warning.

Chapter XCIX

Trouble is coming for those who act wickedly and take pride in their lies, treating them as if they were something good. You will be destroyed, and you will never know true happiness or peace.

Trouble is coming for those who twist the truth, break the eternal laws, and choose a sinful path instead of what they were meant to be. Because of their choices, they will be crushed underfoot, and their own actions will bring about their downfall.

During that time, you who are righteous, be ready to lift up your prayers as a reminder before the angels. Let them bring a record of the sins of the wicked before the Most High, so that their deeds are not forgotten.

In those days, nations will be in chaos, and families will rise up against each other when destruction comes. The world will be filled with disorder. Even the poor will abandon their children, carrying them away only to leave them behind. Infants still nursing will be left without mercy, and parents will show no love even to those they once cherished.

I swear to you, sinners, that a time is coming when sin will lead to endless violence. Bloodshed will not stop, and destruction will continue without end.

Those who bow down to lifeless idols—made of gold, silver, wood, or clay—or who worship unclean spirits and demons will find no help from them. These false gods will not save them.

Because of their foolishness, these people will become blind to the truth. Fear will fill their hearts, and their dreams will be filled with terrifying visions. Instead of leading them to wisdom, these dreams will drive them further into lies and sin. They will spend their lives believing in what is false, worshiping mere stones, and in the end, they will be destroyed in an instant.

But during that time, those who accept and understand the words of wisdom will be blessed. Those who walk in the ways of the Most High, following His path and refusing to join in the sins of the wicked, will find safety and salvation.

Trouble is coming for those who harm their neighbors. They will meet their end in the place of the dead.

Trouble is coming for those who cheat and deceive others, spreading injustice and bitterness throughout the world. Their evil will lead to their complete destruction.

Trouble is coming for those who build their homes through the suffering and unfair labor of others. Their houses are built on sin, and I tell you, they will never find peace.

Trouble is coming for those who turn away from the heritage of their ancestors, choosing instead to follow false gods. They will never find rest for their souls.

Trouble is coming for those who commit evil, support oppression, and kill without remorse. When the great day of judgment comes, their own actions will condemn them.

On that day, the Lord will strip away your power, and your hearts will be filled with fear and suffering. His anger will rise against you, and He will destroy you with the sword. The holy and righteous will remember what you have done, and your shame will never be erased.

Chapter C

In those days, in a single place, fathers and sons will be killed together, and brothers will turn against each other until rivers run red with blood. No one will stop their hand from violence—not even a father will spare his own child, and sinners will kill even those they once respected. From morning until night, they will destroy one another.

Horses will be deep in the blood of sinners, and chariots will sink beneath the surface. During this time, the angels will go to hidden places and gather all those responsible for spreading sin. On that day of judgment, the Most High will rise and bring justice upon the wicked.

For those who are righteous and holy, He will send His angels to protect them like a precious treasure. These angels will guard them until all evil and sin are wiped away. Even if the righteous rest in death for a long time, they will have nothing to fear.

The people on earth will see how the wise are kept safe, and they will finally understand the truth written in this book. They will realize that their wealth cannot protect them from judgment and will not save them from the consequences of their sins.

Trouble is coming for you, sinners, on the day of great suffering. You who have tortured the righteous and burned them will be repaid for all the evil you have done. Trouble is coming for those who are cruel and spend their nights planning wickedness. Fear will fall upon you, and no one will come to help.

Trouble is coming for you, sinners, because of your lies and the evil you have done with your hands. Your own godless actions will bring your destruction, and you will burn in a fire more intense than any flame on earth.

Know this: the Most High will hold even the angels accountable for your sins. He will question the sun, moon, and stars about your wrongdoing, for you have judged the righteous unfairly on earth. He will call upon the clouds, mist, dew, and rain to testify against you, for they will stop falling because of your wickedness, and they will remember your sins.

Go ahead—offer gifts to the rain if you believe that will make it fall. But even silver and gold will not bring back the dew or the rain. When frost, snow, and icy storms come upon you with all their harshness, you will have no strength to withstand them, and you will not be able to escape.

Chapter CI

Look up at the sky, you who belong to heaven, and see everything the Most High has made. Let it fill you with wonder and respect for Him, and do not do evil in His sight.

If He decided to close the heavens and stop the rain and dew from falling because of your actions, what would you do? If He became angry with you because of your sins, there would be no way to plead with Him. You have spoken proud and arrogant words against His righteousness, and because of this, you will never find peace.

Think about the sailors on their ships. Their vessels are tossed around by the waves, shaken by strong winds, and put in great danger. They are terrified because all their valuable possessions are with them on the sea. Their hearts are troubled, fearing the sea will swallow them, taking both their lives and their goods.

Isn't the great sea, with all its waters and waves, created by the Most High? Hasn't He set its boundaries, keeping it in place with the sands of the shore? At His command, the sea trembles and dries up, and all the creatures in it perish. Yet, even after seeing His power, you sinners on the earth do not fear Him.

Didn't He create the heavens and the earth and everything in them? Isn't He the one who gives wisdom and understanding to every living creature on land and in the sea?

Even sailors, who spend their lives on the ocean, are afraid of its power. But you sinners do not fear the Most High, who is far greater than the sea and all its strength.

Chapter CII

In those days, when the Most High sends a fire to consume you, where will you run? Where will you find safety? When He speaks His judgment against you, won't you be filled with fear and terror?

The stars and heavenly lights will tremble in fear. The earth will shake, overwhelmed by the power of His presence. The angels will carry out their duties, but even they will try to hide from the Great Glory. The people of the earth will be filled with terror, and you sinners will be cursed forever. You will never find peace.

But do not be afraid, you who are righteous. Have hope, even if you have died while living a good life. Do not lose heart if your soul has entered the grave in sorrow, or if your body suffered in life despite your righteousness. Wait for the day when judgment will come upon sinners—the day of their punishment.

Even when you die, sinners will mock you, saying, "The righteous die just like we do. What do they gain from their goodness? Look, they die in pain and darkness, just like us. How are they any better? In the end, we are the same. What reward will they get? Will they see anything different after death? They are gone forever, just like we will be."

But I say to you, sinners: You spend your lives feasting, drinking, stealing, sinning, taking advantage of others, and chasing after riches. You enjoy moments of ease and comfort. Have you ever stopped to think about the end of the righteous? Even as they face death, there is no violence in them.

Yet you say, "They are gone as if they never existed. Their spirits have entered the grave, full of sorrow."

Chapter CIII

Now, I make a promise to you who live righteously. I swear by the glory of the Great and Mighty One, the ruler of all things. By His power, I tell you the truth: I have discovered a mystery and read from the heavenly records. I have seen the holy books, and they contain words written about you.

It is written that goodness, joy, and honor have been prepared for you. These blessings are set aside for the spirits of those who have died in righteousness. Great rewards will be given to you for your hard work, and what you receive will be far greater than what the living have. The spirits of those who lived righteously will rejoice and never be forgotten. Their memory will always remain before the Great One for all time. So do not fear the insults or judgment of others.

But trouble is coming for you sinners when you die, especially if you die surrounded by the riches of your wrongdoing. Woe to those who praise you, saying, "Blessed are the sinners! They enjoyed their lives and died in wealth and comfort. They never suffered hardship or faced violence. They were honored in death, and no judgment was brought against them while they lived."

Know this: their souls will descend into Sheol, where they will suffer greatly. They will be chained in darkness, tormented by fire, and sentenced to endless judgment. Every generation of sinners will face this same fate. There will be no peace for them.

Do not lose hope, you who are righteous. Do not say, "In these hard times, we have worked tirelessly, endured suffering, and faced nothing but evil. We have become fewer in number, and our spirits are crushed. We have been defeated and found no one to help us. No kind words were spoken to us. We were tormented and pushed down, losing all hope for a better life. We wanted to lead, but instead, we became the lowest of all. We worked without reward and became prey to sinners and the wicked. They burdened us, ruled over us with cruelty, and struck us without mercy. Even when we bowed before them in submission, they showed no kindness."

Do not despair and say, "We longed to escape their oppression and find rest, but there was no safe place. We cried out to those in power, pleading for justice against those who devoured us, but no one listened. Instead, they helped the wicked, those who robbed and oppressed us. They ignored our suffering and refused to remove the heavy burden from our shoulders. They covered up the murders of our people and erased the violence they committed against us."

Take courage, for the Lord sees everything, and His judgment will not fail.

Chapter CIV

I promise you that the angels in heaven remember you with kindness before the glory of the Great One. Your names are written in His presence. Have hope, because even though you once suffered shame and hardship, you will soon shine like the stars in the sky. You will glow brightly, and everyone will see you, for the gates of heaven will be opened to you.

Call out for justice, and it will come. Everything you have endured will be repaid to those who ruled over you and those who took from you. Do not lose hope, but look forward to great joy, just as the angels in heaven rejoice. What will be expected of you on that day? Nothing—because you will not need to hide when judgment comes. You will not be counted among the sinners, and eternal punishment will be far from you, stretching across all generations.

Do not be afraid, you who live righteously, when you see sinners growing in power and success. Do not follow their ways or get involved in their violence. Instead, your place will be with the heavenly beings. And even though sinners may say, "No one will ever know about our sins, and they will never be written down," understand that every single sin is recorded daily.

Let me show you something: light and darkness, day and night—they all witness what you do. Do not let wickedness grow in your heart. Do not lie, twist the truth, or speak against the Holy and Great One. Do not put your trust in idols. Every act of dishonesty, deceit, and sin does not lead to righteousness, but to even greater wrongdoing.

I know this truth: sinners will twist and change the words of righteousness in many ways. They will spread lies, create deception, and even write books to support their false teachings. But when my words are written down correctly in their own languages—without being changed or distorted—everything I have spoken will remain as it was meant to be.

There is something else I must tell you. Books will be given to the righteous and the wise. These books will bring them joy, understanding, and truth. They will read them, believe in them, and celebrate their wisdom. Through these books, the righteous will learn the right way to live and will be rewarded for their faith and knowledge.

Chapter CV

In those days, the Lord gave a command for wisdom to be shared with the people of the earth. He said, "Teach them, for you are their guides and the ones who will lead them across the whole world. My Son and I will always be with them as they follow the path of righteousness throughout their lives. Peace will be with you. Rejoice, you who live rightly. So be it."

The Fragments of the
Book of Noah

Chapter CVI

After some time, Methuselah found a wife for his son Lamech, and she became pregnant and gave birth to a son. His skin was as white as snow and had a rosy glow like a blooming flower. His hair was long and as white as wool, and his eyes were beautiful. When he opened them, the entire house lit up as if the sun itself was shining inside, filling the room with a brilliant light.

The baby sat up in the midwife's hands, opened his mouth, and spoke words of praise to the Lord of righteousness. Lamech, his father, was so shocked and afraid that he ran to his own father, Methuselah, and said, "I have had a son unlike any other. He doesn't look like an ordinary child—he looks like one of the sons of God. His appearance is different from ours. His eyes shine like the sun, and his face is radiant. I fear that something incredible is going to happen on earth in his lifetime. Please, father, go to our ancestor Enoch and find out the truth, for he lives with the angels."

Methuselah listened to Lamech and set out to find me, Enoch, at the farthest reaches of the earth, for he had heard I was there. When he arrived, he called out to me, and I heard his voice. I went to him and asked, "Here I am, my son. Why have you come?"

He answered, "I am troubled by something urgent and disturbing. My son Lamech has had a child, but he is unlike any other I have ever seen. His skin is whiter than snow and red like a rose. His hair is as white as wool, and his eyes shine like beams of sunlight. When he opened them, the whole house filled with light. He sat up in the midwife's hands, spoke, and praised the Lord of heaven. Lamech is terrified, thinking the child is not his but one of the angels. I have come to you so you can reveal the truth."

I, Enoch, replied, "The Lord is going to do something new on the earth. I have seen it in a vision, and I will tell you what I know. In the time of my father Jared, some angels of heaven disobeyed the Lord. They broke His laws and took human women as their wives, having children with them. Because of this, great destruction will come upon the earth. A massive flood will cover the land for an entire year. But this child that has been born to Lamech will survive. He and his three sons will be saved, while the rest of the world perishes.

From his descendants will come people who are not spiritual but of the flesh, and because of their ways, the earth will suffer great judgment. The world will be cleansed of its wickedness. Go back and tell your son Lamech that this child is indeed his. He should name him Noah, for he will live through the great destruction along with his sons. This judgment is coming because of the sin and corruption that will grow to its peak in his time.

But after this flood, even greater wickedness will arise. I have seen it in the mysteries of the holy ones. The Lord has revealed these things to me, and I have read them on the heavenly tablets."

Chapter CVII

1. I saw written that generation after generation will continue to sin until one generation of righteousness appears. When that time comes, wrongdoing will be removed, sin will disappear from the earth, and goodness will fill the world.

2. Now, my son, go and tell your son Lamech that this child who has been born is truly his. There is no mistake about it.

3. When Methuselah heard his father Enoch's words—because

Enoch had revealed everything to him in secret—he returned to Lamech and told him everything. Then he named the child Noah, for he would bring comfort to the earth after all the destruction.

The Book of the Heavenly Luminaries

Chapter LXXI

This book explains how the lights in the sky move, their purpose, and how they change with the seasons throughout the year. Uriel, the holy angel who guided me, explained everything carefully. He showed me how these lights follow their set rules, continuing this way forever until a new creation begins that will last for eternity.

The first rule of the lights in the sky is this: The sun rises through the eastern gates of heaven and sets through the western gates.

I saw six openings in the east where the sun rises and six in the west where it sets. The moon and stars also use these same gates, following their assigned paths. There are six main gates in the east and six in the west, all working together perfectly in an orderly system. Besides these, there are also many smaller openings to the right and left.

The greatest light in the sky is the sun. It appears as large as the entire sky, shining brightly with fire, giving both light and warmth to the world. The sun moves across the sky, carried by the wind. At the end of the day, it descends and travels through the northern regions, returning to the east to start its journey again at the right time.

The Sun's Path Throughout the Year

In the first month, the sun rises through the fourth eastern gate. This gate has twelve smaller openings that release fiery light at certain times. The sun continues to rise from this fourth gate for thirty days, setting each evening through the fourth western gate.

During this time, the days grow longer, and the nights become shorter. By the thirtieth day, the daylight lasts one-ninth longer than the nighttime. The day is divided into ten parts, and the night into eight parts.

After this, the sun moves to the fifth gate in the east, rising from there for thirty more days. As the cycle continues, daylight increases, reaching eleven parts, while the night shortens to seven parts.

Next, the sun enters the sixth eastern gate, where it rises and sets for thirty-one days. At this point, the daytime is twice as long as the nighttime. The day is now twelve parts, while the night is six parts.

After reaching this peak, the days start getting shorter, and the nights become longer again. The sun then begins its journey back, following the same gates but in reverse order.

The sun returns to the sixth eastern gate, rising there for thirty days before shifting back to the fifth gate for another thirty days. As this happens, the daylight decreases, and the nighttime grows longer.

When the sun reaches the fourth gate again, the length of the day and night become equal, each lasting nine parts.

The cycle continues as the sun moves through the third eastern gate, rising from there for thirty days, and setting in the third western gate each evening.

This pattern repeats every year, showing the precise order and harmony of the sun's movement, following its path without change.

On this day, the night begins to grow longer than the day. With each passing evening, the night keeps increasing, while the day becomes shorter. This pattern continues until the thirtieth day. At that point, the night lasts ten parts, while the day is reduced to eight parts.

The sun keeps moving along its set path, rising from the third portal in the east and setting in the third portal in the west. Then, it moves to the second portal, where it rises for thirty more mornings and sets each evening through the second western portal, following the same pattern.

As this phase continues, the night grows even longer. On this day, the night reaches eleven parts, while the day shortens to seven parts. The sun, staying true to its course, rises again from the second portal in the east and sets in the second portal in the west.

Then, the sun moves to the first eastern portal, where it rises for thirty-one mornings and sets each night through the first western portal. This marks a key transition in the cycle of light and darkness.

On the final day of this phase, the night reaches its longest length, becoming twice as long as the day. At this point, the night lasts twelve full parts, while the day is reduced to six parts. Everything follows its precise order, just as it was set from the beginning.

The sun completes its journey through the divisions of its orbit, reaching its farthest point. Then, it starts to move back, rising from the same eastern portal for thirty more mornings and setting in the opposite western portal.

During this phase, the nights start getting shorter again. By the end of this period, the night decreases by one-ninth, meaning the night now lasts eleven parts, while the day grows to seven parts.

The sun then returns to the second eastern portal, rising from there for thirty days. As this continues, the night gets even shorter, now lasting ten parts, while the day increases to eight parts.

Next, the sun moves to the third eastern portal, rising there for thirty-one mornings and setting in the third western portal. By the end of this phase, day and night become equal again. Now, both day and night last nine parts each, and the year reaches exactly 364 days.

This balance happens because of the sun's movement. The length of the day and night changes based on where the sun is along its path. Each part of the year follows a set order, keeping the cycle of light and darkness perfectly in balance.

The sun's journey completes its full cycle sixty times in total, marking the entire year. This great light, the sun, moves without stopping, shining on the world forever and ever. It follows its path precisely, never changing, never resting, as it travels across the sky.

The sun's light is seven times brighter than the moon's light, making it the strongest source of brightness in the sky. However, both the sun and the moon are the same size. This perfect balance shows the order and precision of creation, as it was set by the Lord.

Because of this, the sun's rising and setting remain a constant sign of the harmony in the heavens, a pattern that continues forever without end.

Chapter LXXII

After learning about the sun's movement, I turned my attention to another light in the sky—the moon. The moon is large, stretching across the sky like the heavens themselves. Like the sun, it is carried across the sky by the wind, following its own set path. However, unlike the sun, the moon's light is measured and given in small portions, causing it to change shape throughout the month.

The moon's rising and setting shift every month, creating a pattern different from the sun's. Though its days are similar in length, its light is much softer, only one-seventh as bright as the sun when it reaches its fullest phase.

The moon starts its cycle in a unique way. On the thirtieth morning, a small portion of the moon becomes visible in the eastern sky, marking the beginning of its cycle. On this day, it rises in the same place as the sun, showing just a faint sliver of light. Most of its surface remains dark, and only one-seventh of its full brightness appears.

As the moon gains light, it receives another small portion of brightness. This happens in fractions, increasing little by little.

The moon often follows the sun, rising and setting at similar times. When the sun rises in the morning, the moon also rises, receiving a small additional amount of light. However, during the start of the lunar cycle, the moon is nearly invisible because it is so close to the sun. At this time, its light is very faint, making it difficult to see.

As days pass, the moon becomes easier to notice. One morning, it rises with exactly one-seventh of its light showing. From there, it slowly moves away from the sun's rising point. In the following days, its brightness continues to grow, lighting up more and more of its surface. Each phase follows a precise and steady pattern, revealing the careful order of the moon's movement in the sky.

Chapter LXXIII

I observed another cycle, this time focusing on the Moon and how it follows a set path each month. This pattern controls how the Moon moves, changes shape, and sets. Uriel, the holy angel who leads the lights in the sky, explained this cycle to me, showing me where the Moon travels and how its light changes over fifteen days. I carefully wrote down everything he showed me, including the months, the brightness of the Moon, and how it fades and grows.

The Moon's light increases little by little, growing in the east in seventh parts. Then, in the west, it fades away in the same steady pattern until it becomes completely dark. This process repeats every month, but in certain months, the Moon shifts its setting, following a slightly different path.

In two months of the year, the Moon sets at the same time as the Sun, passing through the middle portals—the third and fourth gates. For seven days, it moves outward, then returns to the same portal where the Sun rises, reaching full brightness. After that, the Moon starts moving away from the Sun and, over eight days, enters the sixth portal, which is also where the Sun rises.

As the Sun moves out of the fourth portal, the Moon keeps traveling, staying visible for seven days before shifting into the fifth portal. Then, it reverses its course and returns to the fourth portal within seven days, again reaching full brightness. After that, it moves further back, entering the first portal after another eight days.

The Moon continues this precise cycle, staying in sync with the Sun's movement. I carefully observed how the Moon's setting was always connected to where the Sun was positioned during these times.

Over time, I learned that when five years are counted together, the Sun completes an extra thirty days. This happens because, every year in this five-year cycle, the Sun, stars, and Moon work together to make a total of 364 days. However, the Moon moves slightly slower than the Sun and stars, falling thirty days behind over the same five-year period.

The Sun and stars move with perfect accuracy, never getting ahead or falling behind by even a single day. Every year, they complete their cycles exactly, keeping a perfect total of 364 days. Over three years, this adds up to 1,092 days. In five years, it reaches 1,820 days, and after eight years, the count grows to 2,912 days.

The Moon, however, falls behind slightly. In three years, its total is 1,062 days. After five years, it is fifty days short of the Sun and stars, making its total 1,770 days. In eight years, the Moon's total reaches 2,832 days, meaning it falls eighty days behind over that time.

Even though the Moon's cycle is slightly different, the overall yearly pattern stays perfectly balanced. The Sun and Moon continue to rise and set from their assigned places, following a steady pattern of thirty days per month. This perfect design of the heavens keeps everything moving in order, ensuring that the cycles remain stable and never change.

Chapter LXXIV

The leaders of the heavenly order, who guide the countless stars and celestial bodies, are also responsible for four special days that are separate from the rest of the year. These four days play an important role in keeping time, even though they are not included in the official count of the year's days. The sun, moon, and stars follow their cycles during these days, but because their effects are not easy to see, people often misunderstand their purpose.

These four special days are linked to specific positions in the sky where the sun rises and sets at key times of the year. The first is in the first portal, the second in the third, the third in the fourth, and the last in the sixth portal. These positions help maintain the accuracy of the 364-day cycle that structures the year.

Uriel, the holy angel, explained these mysteries to me. The Lord of Glory gave him the job of watching over all the lights in the sky, controlling their movements across the heavens and the earth. These heavenly lights, including the sun, moon, and stars, rule over day and night, while other heavenly forces—like chariots of light—move in harmony with them.

Uriel also showed me twelve great doors surrounding the sun's chariot in the sky. These doors open and close at specific times, allowing the sun's rays to shine on the earth, bringing light and warmth. The way these doors open and close controls the changing of the seasons, showing the careful design behind creation.

He also explained how the winds and morning dew have their own openings in the sky. These portals, located at the edges of the heavens, allow natural forces to flow as part of their cycle. The sun, moon, and stars move through twelve gateways at the ends of the earth, ensuring their correct rising and setting in both the east and west.

Near these gateways, there are many windows on either side. Each window opens at a specific time, releasing warmth or light to the earth as instructed. These windows work together with the star portals, controlling the timing and placement of heavenly light.

As I looked toward the heavens, I saw chariots in constant motion, moving along their paths above the portals. These chariots guide the stars that never set, keeping them in their designated orbits. Among them was one massive chariot, larger than all the rest. It moved across the entire sky, playing a major role in the divine system that governs the heavens.

Through these twelve portals and their many windows, I saw the wisdom and precision of the Creator. Every part of the heavens follows its assigned path, working perfectly in harmony with the design set in place from the very beginning.

Chapter LXXV

At the farthest edges of the earth, I saw twelve large openings in the sky. These were the gateways for the winds, allowing them to move across the earth and affect everything on it. Each gateway was positioned in a specific direction, controlling how the winds traveled.

Three of these portals faced east, releasing the first set of winds. Another three were in the west, carrying their own effects. The next three were in the south, and the last three in the north. Together, these twelve portals formed a complete system, sending both helpful and harmful winds across the land and sea.

The winds were divided into two types:

- Four winds brought blessings, bringing rain, health, and good harvests to the earth.
- The other eight were destructive, spreading drought, storms, and disasters that harmed the land, water, and living creatures.

The east winds came from three portals:

- The first eastern wind blew slightly southward and was harsh and destructive, bringing drought, extreme heat, and ruin.
- The second eastern wind, coming from the middle portal, was gentle and nourishing, bringing rain, dew, and fruitful harvests.
- The third eastern wind, leaning northward, was cold and often caused dry conditions.

The south winds came from their own three portals:

- The first southern wind, coming from the eastward side, was hot and dry.
- The second southern wind, from the middle portal, carried pleasant scents, dew, rain, and good health.
- The third southern wind, blowing from the westward side, brought dew and rain but also swarms of locusts, which could either nourish the land or cause destruction.

Then I observed the north winds:

- The first northern wind, coming from the eastern side, brought dew and rain but also locusts and ruin.
- The second northern wind, from the middle portal, carried rain, dew, and blessings of good health.
- The third northern wind, from the western side, brought a mix of clouds, frost, snow, rain, and locusts, sometimes helping the land and other times harming it.

Finally, I looked at the west winds:

- The first western wind, from the northern side, carried dew, frost, cold, and snow.
- The second western wind, from the middle portal, brought dew, rain, and prosperity.
- The third western wind, from the southern side, was harsh and burning, bringing drought, destruction, and scorching heat.

These twelve portals, spread across the four directions, controlled the winds that affect the world. Each one followed its own rules, shaping both blessings and disasters for the earth. These mysteries of the winds and their effects were shown to me, and I am sharing them with you, my son Methuselah, so that you may understand the balance and order in creation. The way these winds work reveals the complex and precise design of the world.

Chapter LXXVI

The first direction is called the east because it is where everything begins. The second direction is the south, where the Most High will one day come down in a special and meaningful way. The Blessed One, who exists forever, will descend to this place.

The west is known as the fading quarter because this is where all the heavenly lights complete their journey and disappear from view.

The fourth direction, the north, is divided into three parts:

1. The first section is where people live.

2. The second section contains huge bodies of water, including seas, deep valleys, thick forests, flowing rivers, and areas covered in darkness and heavy clouds.

3. The third section is where the Garden of Righteousness is found—a place of great beauty and holiness.

I also saw seven towering mountains, taller than any other mountains on earth. From these mountains comes hoarfrost, which helps mark the passing of days, the changing seasons, and the turning of years.

There were also seven great rivers, larger than any others on earth.

- One flows from the west and empties into the Great Sea.

- Two come from the north and flow into the Erythraean Sea in the east.
- The remaining four also start in the north: two flow into the Erythraean Sea, while the other two empty into the Great Sea. Some say that parts of these waters may also flow into the desert.

I also saw seven large islands, spread between the land and the seas.

- Two of these islands are on the mainland.
- The other five are in the Great Sea.

Chapter LXXVII

The sun has two names: Orjares and Tomas. The moon has four names: Asonja, Ebla, Benase, and Erae. These two are the great lights in the sky, and they are the same size and shape, stretching across the heavens. However, the sun is much brighter because it holds seven extra portions of light. These portions are transferred little by little until all seven are fully given.

Both the sun and the moon set in the west and continue their journey through the north before rising again in the east, lighting up the sky. When the moon appears, only one-fourteenth of her light is visible. Her brightness grows each day, and by the fourteenth day, she is fully lit. On the fifteenth day, her light reaches its peak, divided into fifteen parts. This cycle follows a set pattern every year, with the moon's light increasing steadily each day.

As the moon begins to shrink, her light fades little by little.

- On the first day of waning, her light reduces to fourteen parts.
- On the second day, it shrinks to thirteen parts.
- On the third day, only twelve parts remain, and this continues each day.

By the fourteenth day of waning, only a tiny fraction of her light is left—half of one-seventh part. By the fifteenth day, her light disappears completely, leaving the moon dark.

In some months, the moon's cycle lasts twenty-nine days, while in others, it is twenty-eight days.

Uriel, the holy angel, also explained how the moon gets her light from the sun. When the moon is waxing, she gathers light from the sun while standing opposite it. Over fourteen days, her light becomes complete, and when she is fully lit, she shines brightly across the sky.

The first day of her cycle is called the new moon because that is when she begins to shine. She becomes a full moon on the same day the sun sets in the west. That night, she rises in the east, shining through the entire night until the sun rises again in the morning. At this moment, the moon stands directly opposite the sun.

As the moon fades, her light shrinks from the side it first appeared on. This continues until her light disappears completely and she becomes dark. When her cycle ends, the month is complete.

- For three months, the moon's cycle lasts thirty days.
- For another three months, her cycle lasts twenty-nine days.
- In these months, the full and fading moon phases are completed in 177 days.

When the moon reappears, she follows the same pattern again.

- She shines for three months of thirty days.
- Then, she shines for three months of twenty-nine days.

During the night, she takes on a shape that resembles a person for twenty days in each cycle. But during the day, she blends into the sky, and only her light is visible.

Chapter LXXVIII

Now, my son, I have explained everything to you, and the rules that govern all the stars in the sky are now complete.

He showed me how each of them moves, explaining their patterns for every day, every season, and how they take turns shining in the sky. He also revealed their yearly cycles, the paths they follow, and how they are arranged for each month and each week.

I was also shown how the moon fades over time, beginning in the sixth portal. At this point, the moon reaches full brightness, and from there, it starts to lose light.

As the moon continues its cycle, it moves through the first portal, following its seasonal pattern until 177 days have passed. These 177 days are divided into twenty-five weeks and two extra days.

Throughout this cycle, the moon lags behind the sun and the stars' patterns by exactly five days in a full period. This delay becomes noticeable once she completes her journey along the path you see.

This is the full explanation of how all the lights in the sky move, as revealed to me by Uriel, the archangel, who leads and watches over them all.

Chapter LXXIX

During that time, the angel Uriel spoke to me and said, "Enoch, I have now shown you everything. You have seen how the sun and moon move, how the stars follow their paths, and how everything in the heavens follows a set order. I have explained their duties, schedules, and how they appear and disappear according to the laws of the universe.

But when sinners fill the earth, the natural order will break down. The years will be shortened, and people will struggle to plant and harvest at the right times. The land will stop producing crops, and the seasons will no longer follow their normal cycle. Rain will stop falling, and the sky will hold back its water.

Fruits will not grow as they should, and harvests will be delayed. The trees will stop producing fruit on time, and nothing will ripen when expected.

Even the moon will change its cycle. It will no longer appear at the right times, and its phases will be thrown off balance. The sun will also behave strangely, shining brighter than usual and following a different path, moving too far west in its great journey across the sky.

Some stars will rebel against their assigned courses, ignoring their duties and schedules. They will move in unpredictable ways, failing to appear when they should. The entire order of the heavens will seem hidden from people, and those on earth will lose their understanding of the stars. Instead of recognizing their true purpose, people will fall into confusion and begin worshiping them as gods.

As evil increases, so will the punishment. Sin will multiply, and in the end, judgment will come upon the wicked, leading to their destruction."

Chapter LXXX

He said to me, "Enoch, look closely at these heavenly tablets. Read everything written on them and pay attention to every detail so you can understand their full meaning."

I focused on the tablets and read everything recorded there. I saw and understood it all—the complete history of humanity, including the actions of every person who would ever live, from the past to the distant future. The knowledge was deep and overwhelming.

Right away, I praised the great Lord, the eternal King of glory, who created everything. I thanked Him for His patience and kindness toward people, amazed by His greatness and mercy, which are beyond understanding.

Then I said, "Blessed is the one who lives and dies in righteousness, for no record of wrongdoing will be written against them. They will not face judgment. How fortunate are those who are free from sin and guilt in the eyes of the Lord!"

After that, the seven holy ones who had guided me brought me back to earth. They placed me in front of my home and said, "Enoch, share everything you have learned with your son Methuselah. Teach him and all your children, for no one is truly righteous before the Lord. He is their Creator, and He knows everything they do.

You have one year left to spend with your family. Use this time to teach them, write down everything you have seen, and pass on the wisdom you have learned. In the second year, you will be taken away and will no longer live among them."

They continued, "Stay strong, for the righteous will support one another. The good will rejoice with the good, encouraging each other. But sinners will be destroyed along with other sinners, and those who reject the truth will share the fate of others like them.

The righteous may suffer or even die because of the wicked, and they may be taken away because of the sins of others. But their reward is safe, for the Lord sees their faithfulness."

After they finished speaking, they left me, and I returned to my people. My heart was full of gratitude and respect for the Lord. I blessed Him for all He had revealed and for His unending justice and mercy.

Chapter LXXXI

Now, my son Methuselah, I am sharing all these things with you and writing them down so you can keep them safe. I have told you everything and entrusted you with these books, which contain the wisdom and knowledge I have received. Take care of these books, my son, and make sure they are passed down to future generations so that those who come after you can also learn from them.

I have given you wisdom, not just for yourself, but for your children and their descendants. This wisdom is meant to be passed down through the generations. It contains truths that go beyond what most people understand, offering insight into the mysteries of creation. Those who seek this wisdom will stay alert, eager to learn more. They will listen carefully and find joy in this knowledge, seeing it as more satisfying than the finest food.

Blessed are those who live righteously, following the ways of justice and avoiding the paths of sin. They live in harmony with the order of the heavens, just as the sun follows its path across the sky. The sun moves through its portals, staying in each for thirty days at a time, guided by the heavenly leaders who oversee the stars. Four special days are added to divide the year into its four seasons, following the order set by the heavens. However, people often forget to count these extra days and make mistakes in calculating the total length of the year.

These four extra days are an important part of the year's cycle and are recorded forever in the heavenly tablets. One belongs to the first portal, another to the third, the next to the fourth, and the last to the sixth portal. Together, they complete the year, which is exactly 364 days long. This count is accurate and was revealed to me by Uriel, the archangel. Uriel, appointed by the Lord of all creation, watches over the movements of the sun, moon, and stars, making sure they follow their proper courses.

Uriel controls the changes between day and night in the heavens, making sure that light reaches the earth through the sun, moon, and stars. These celestial bodies move in their paths, carried by their heavenly chariots. The stars follow specific patterns, appearing at the right times during different seasons, festivals, and months. Each one fulfills its purpose according to the divine plan.

There are leaders among the stars who make sure they shine at the right times. They take turns ruling during their seasons and periods of influence. There are four leaders who divide the year into its four quarters, followed by twelve leaders who oversee the months. Others manage the 360 days of the year, along with the four extra days that divide the year into its proper parts.

The leaders who divide the year are Milki'el, Hel'emmelek, Mel'ejael, and Narel. Assisting them are others like Adnarel, Ijasusael, and Elomeel. These leaders make sure the stars and seasons follow their correct order. Each has a specific role, and they take turns leading in a precise sequence.

At the beginning of the year, Melkejâl rises first. He is also known as Tam'âini, and he rules for ninety-one days. During his time, the earth experiences warmth, calm weather, and the growth of new life. Trees bear fruit, leaves sprout, and the wheat harvest is gathered. Flowers like roses bloom in the fields, while the trees from winter begin to wither. Under Melkejâl's rule are Berka'el, Zelebs'el, and another leader named Hilujaseph. When their ninety-one days end, their time of rule is over.

After them, Hel'emmelek takes over. Known as "the shining sun," he also rules for ninety-one days. During his time, the earth feels intense heat and dryness. Fruits ripen, sheep mate and become pregnant, and the harvest is gathered, including grapes being pressed for wine. The earth's abundance is collected during his time. The leaders under Hel'emmelek are Gida'ijal, Ke'el, He'el, and another leader named Asfa'el. After these ninety-one days, their rule also comes to an end.

These leaders, their schedules, and their appointed times show the careful design of the heavens and the earth, revealing the divine order that governs everything.

Thank You for Reading

Dear Reader,

We hope this timeless classic has sparked your imagination and enriched your literary journey. Now that you've turned the final page, we want to share a vision for the future of reading—one where every classic you've ever wanted to explore is at your fingertips, in a format that best suits your life.

We'd like to invite you to gain immediate, unlimited digital & audiobook access to hundreds of the most treasured literary classics ever written—along with the option to secure deluxe paperback, hardcover & box set editions at printing cost. Together, we can spark a new global literary renaissance alongside our small, independent publishing house called "The Library of Alexandria."

Thousands of years ago, the Library of Alexandria stood as a beacon of knowledge—until it was lost to history. We aim to reignite that spirit of preservation and discovery right now, in the modern age—only this time, it's accessible to all, in every language and every format.

Picture a world where every timeless classic, novel, poem, or philosophical treatise is not only available to read but also updated for today's readers—modernized, translated into any language or dialect, and ready to enjoy in any format you choose, whether that is in an eBook, audiobook, paperback, or deluxe hardcover & box set version a printing cost.

By joining our movement to rebuild the modern Library of Alexandria, you become part of an unprecedented mission to offer:

- **Unlimited Audiobook & eBook Access to the Greatest Classics of All Time**

Instantly explore thousands of legendary works, from Plato and Shakespeare to Jane Austen and Leo Tolstoy. All are instantly ready to read or listen to, giving you a complete literary universe at your fingertips.

- **Paperback & Deluxe Editions at Printing Costs:**

Purchase any title in a paperback, deluxe hardbound, or deluxe boxset edition at printing costs, shipped right to your doorstep. Curate your personal library of Alexandria with editions worthy of display—crafted to last, designed to captivate, and delivered straight to your door.

- **Modern translations for Contemporary Readers in all languages and dialects**

Discover a vast selection of classics reimagined in clear, current language—no more struggling with outdated phrases or obscure references. Next to the original versions, we aim to offer translations in as many languages and dialects as possible.

As we continue our translation efforts and add new languages, readers everywhere can connect with these works as if they were written today. By bridging linguistic divides, you're contributing to ensuring that these timeless stories become more meaningful, accessible, and inspiring for people across the globe.

- **Your Personal Library of Alexandria:**

Over the months and years, you'll curate a unique physical archive of classics—each volume a testament to your taste, curiosity, and love of knowledge. It's not just about owning books—it's about curating a cultural legacy you'll cherish and pass down for generations to come.

- **Join a Global Literary Renaissance:**

  Your support fuels an ongoing mission: allowing us to reinvest in offering deluxe print editions (including special boxsets) at their true cost, broaden the range of available formats and translations, and extend the reach of these works to new audiences worldwide. By joining today, you're not just preserving a legacy of masterpieces; you set in motion a powerful wave of literary accessibility.

  We are more than a publisher—we're a movement, and we can't do it alone. Your support lets us scale our mission, preserving and reimagining history's greatest works for tomorrow's readers.

Become a Torchbearer of knowledge.

Thank you for picking up this book and allowing us into your literary journey. As you turn the pages, know that you're part of something larger: a global effort to keep these stories alive, share their wisdom across borders and generations, and spark a true cultural revival for the modern era.

If this resonates with you—please consider taking the next step by visiting:

www.libraryofalexandria.com

With gratitude and a shared love of knowledge,

The Modern Library of Alexandria Team

Visit:

www.libraryofalexandria.com

Or scan the code below: